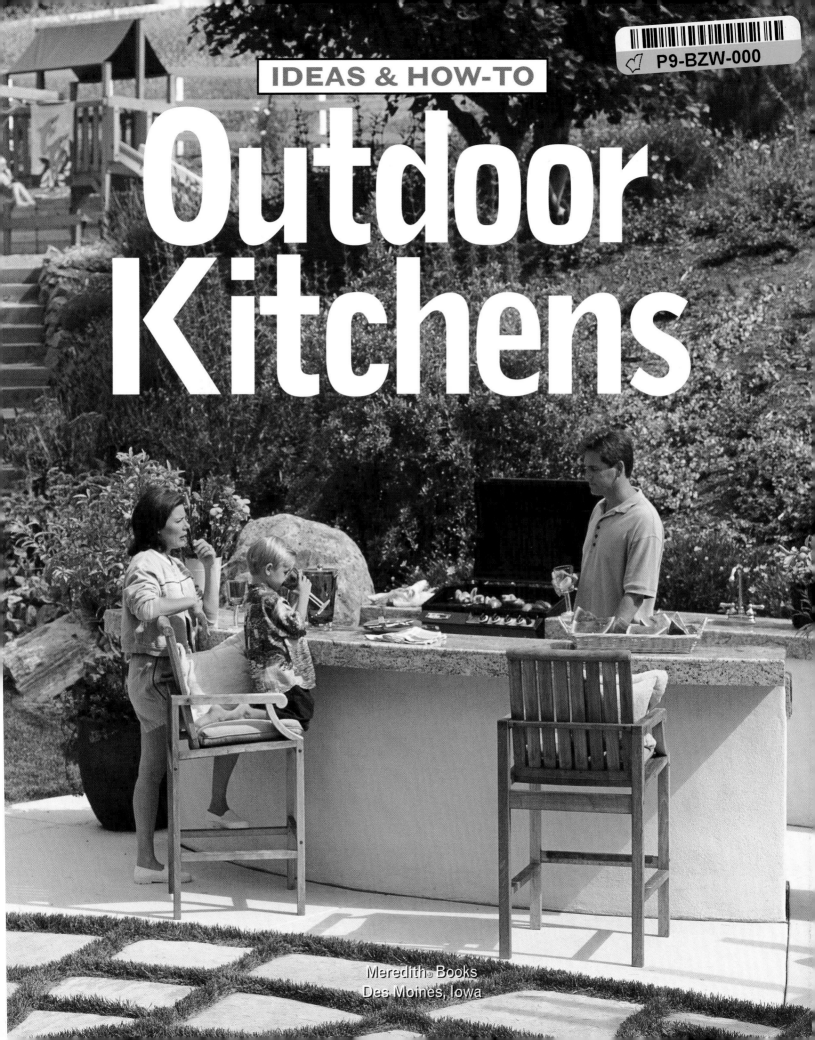

IDEAS & HOW-TO

Outdoor Kitchens

P9-BZW-000

Meredith® Books
Des Moines, Iowa

Better Homes and Gardens® Ideas & How-To: Outdoor Kitchens
Editor: Ken Sidey
Contributing Project Manager/Writer: Dan Weeks
Associate Design Director: Todd Emerson Hanson
Contributing Graphic Designer: Matthew Eberhart,
    Evil Eye Design, Inc.
Copy Chief: Terri Fredrickson
Copy Editor: Kevin Cox
Publishing Operations Manager: Karen Schirm
Senior Editor, Asset & Information Management: Phillip Morgan
Edit and Design Production Coordinator: Mary Lee Gavin
Art and Editorial Sourcing Coordinator: Jackie Swartz
Editorial Assistants: Kaye Chabot, Renee McAtee
Book Production Managers: Pam Kvitne, Marjorie J. Schenkelberg,
    Mark Weaver
Imaging Center Operator: Kristin Reese
Contributing Copy Editor: Joyce Gemperlein
Contributing Proofreaders: Pam Elizian, Judy Friedman, Pam Mohr
Contributing Indexer: Donald Glassman
Contributing Illustrator: Chuck Lockhart

Meredith® Books
Editor in Chief: Gregory H. Kayko
Executive Director, Design: Matt Strelecki
Managing Editor: Amy Tincher-Durik
Executive Editor: Benjamin W. Allen
Senior Editor/Group Manager: Vicki Leigh Ingham
Senior Associate Design Director: Ken Carlson
Marketing Product Manager: Brent Wiersma

Executive Director, Marketing and New Business: Kevin Kacere
Director, Marketing and Publicity: Amy Nichols
Executive Director, Sales: Ken Zagor
Director, Operations: George A. Susral
Director, Production: Douglas M. Johnston
Business Director: Jim Leonard

Senior Vice President: Karla Jeffries
Vice President and General Manager: Douglas J. Guendel

Better Homes and Gardens® **Magazine**
Editor in Chief: Gayle Goodson Butler
Deputy Editor, Home Design: Oma Blaise Ford

Meredith Publishing Group
President: Jack Griffin
Executive Vice President: Doug Olson

Meredith Corporation
Chairman of the Board: William T. Kerr
President and Chief Executive Officer: Stephen M. Lacy

In Memoriam: E.T. Meredith III (1933–2003)

Copyright © 2008 by Meredith Corporation, Des Moines, Iowa.
First Edition.
All rights reserved.
Printed in the United States of America.
Library of Congress Control Number: 2007933340
ISBN: 978-0-696-23543-6

All of us at Meredith® Books are dedicated to providing you with
information and ideas to enhance your home. We welcome your
comments and suggestions. Write to us at: Meredith Books, Home
Decorating and Design Editorial Department, 1716 Locust St., Des
Moines, IA 50309-3023.

Note to the Readers: Due to differing conditions, tools,
and individual skills, Meredith Corporation assumes no
responsibility for any damages, injuries suffered, or losses
incurred as a result of following the information published
in this book. Before beginning any project, review the
instructions carefully, and if any doubts or questions
remain, consult local experts or authorities. Because codes
and regulations vary greatly, you always should check
with authorities to ensure that your project complies with
all applicable local codes and regulations. Always read
and observe all of the safety precautions provided by
manufacturers of any tools, equipment, or supplies, and
follow all accepted safety procedures.

Photographers
(Photographers credited may retain copyright © to the listed photographs.)

L = Left, R = Right, C = Center, B = Bottom, T = Top

Cal Flame: 118BR

DHM Group: 114T

Golich, Ed: 4B, 23R, 56, 57T, 57B, 58–59, 60–61, 89BC

Jensen, Mike: cover

Kamado: 114C

Modern Home Products: 79B

Rockers: 87B

Twin Eagle: 118BC, 119TL

Viking: 10–11, 17, 88, 96–97, 98T???, 98T 3rd from L, 98BR,
    114B, 118TR, 119TR, 119BR, 175B, 186

Walsh, Tony: 62, 63, 64T, 64B, 65, 93, 124–125, 175T

Weber-Stephen: 112, 119BC

Weeks, Dan: 83BL, 84B, 87TL, 87TR, 121TL, 121TR, 121BL,
    143TL, 143TC, 143TR, 148TL, 148TR, 148BL, 148BR, 153,
    155TL, 155TR, 155BL, 155BR, 161TR, 161BL, 161BR, 165BL,
    165BC, 165BR, 169TR, 169BL, 174T, 191

Contents

Introduction

Outdoor kitchens are hot! All it takes is a quick stroll down the aisles of a home center or outdoor living store to spot the trend. Grills are getting bigger and more powerful, and accessories such as side burners and rotisseries are becoming standard equipment on all but the least expensive units. You'll find storage units, weatherized refrigerators, and outdoor sinks—items that required a trip to a specialty retailer just a few years ago. Statistics underscore that consumers are buying into the trend: Recent shipments of outdoor grills have increased at double-digit rates.

The most surprising thing about the rise in outdoor kitchens is that it took so long to get here. Imagine walking into an open house and hearing the real estate agent "boast" that the kitchen offers 18 inches of counterspace, zero storage, and a stove that's just 30 feet from the sink and refrigerator! That's precisely what backyard cooks have endured for years.

This beautifully appointed patio includes all the elements of a great outdoor kitchen: a well-equipped grill, plenty of counterspace and storage, and a sheltered spot for dining.

A modest approach still includes many of the elements of a successful outdoor cooking space. The grill is installed in a small island with storage and counterspace, steps away from a cheerful dining area.

The warmth of a fireplace can extend the enjoyment of an outdoor kitchen well into the cool of the evening.

Outdoor kitchens don't have to be that way. No matter how big or small a budget, you can upgrade a simple grill to create a more functional, enticing, and entertaining place to enjoy your backyard and spend more time with family and friends.

This book is designed to provide you with all the ideas and information you need to create the outdoor kitchen of your dreams. Whether doing it yourself or hiring a team of professionals, you'll find the inspiration to create an outdoor kitchen that blends perfectly with your lifestyle and personality, your home's architecture, and existing backyard. Since outdoor kitchens often are designed in the context of other backyard amenities such as porches, decks, patios, terraces, pools, gardens, and sitting areas, this book addresses integrating many elements into a multifaceted whole.

To make that happen, you'll start by exploring the outdoor kitchen features you need and considering the extras. This assessment process will help you prioritize the elements of your outdoor kitchen.

Next you'll learn the key concepts that professional designers use to create successful outdoor kitchens. You'll discover the impact of location and siting and how to plan your project to make the most of the space you have—be it an expansive suburban backyard or a cozy urban patio.

Later chapters detail the products, accessories, materials, and landscaping that go into an outdoor kitchen. You'll learn how to make the perfect selections for your situation and budget. There's even a chapter on the nitty-gritty details of choosing and working with architects, landscape designers, and contractors, and developing a budget.

As you move through the book, you'll find more than a dozen typical outdoor kitchen projects—from building a simple grill stand to installing a glazed roof over an outdoor kitchen—depicted in photography and cutaway drawings, along with explanations of what goes into executing them. Whether you choose to tackle one of these projects yourself or hire them out, you'll have a good overview of the materials and techniques involved.

Finally you'll find a wealth of outdoor cooking tips and mouthwatering recipes from the experts in the renowned Better Homes and Gardens® Test Kitchen.

An outdoor kitchen can complement other outdoor amenities to create a "backyard resort" that everyone can enjoy.

The heart of any outdoor kitchen is the grill. Added features such as a rotisserie and a side burner expand the range of foods that can be cooked.

1

Assessing Your

If it's necessary, this kitchen has it! It features two professional gas pizza ovens, a big grill, a rotisserie, a large wok burner, and side burners—all in a main island with a storage cabinet fronted by stainless steel. A refrigerator anchors the nearby serving island, and the rolling keg cooler can be positioned wherever it's most handy.

Moving the Kitchen Outdoors

Kitchens rightly have been called "the heart of the home." No longer just a place to put a meal together, today's kitchens serve a variety of roles. In many homes they are the spots where families are most likely to enjoy a few minutes of conversation or gather for breakfast, lunch, or dinner. In the evening the kids might settle in for homework or swing by for a quick snack. On weekends kitchens become casual entertaining centers.

An outdoor kitchen plays many of these same roles, but in a more relaxed—and perhaps more spacious—setting. Warm sunshine, cool breezes, and the sounds of songbirds paint a relaxing backdrop. Far from the TV and telephone, the well-planned backyard kitchen is a refreshing change of scene from the indoor world.

With space for private dining in sun or shade, this deck integrates many of the most valuable features of a well-appointed outdoor kitchen. The cooking zone, in the background, is near enough to be handy but far enough to keep heat and fumes at bay.

PRACTICAL ISSUES

Beyond the psychological benefits an outdoor kitchen offers several practical advantages. Hard-core grilling is nearly impossible indoors. Even a modestly priced gas grill can generate two to three times the heat of a typical indoor range burner. Without a powerful (and very expensive) commercial ventilation hood to suck up fumes and smoke, grilling indoors is not a pleasant chore. The heat alone from a powerful grill would make most kitchens unbearably warm.

In addition, an outdoor kitchen may increase the value of your home. According to the National Association of Home Builders, an increasing number of home buyers are looking for luxury touches such as outdoor kitchens, and signs are that demand is going to increase.

Surrounded by tile counters and a fire-resistant Ipe hardwood frame, the built-in gas grill makes a style statement that complements the home's Craftsman styling.

Permanent shelter from the hot sun and rain (and snow) is the most reliable way to ensure that you use your outdoor kitchen throughout the year. This kitchen's closed roof keeps the chef and diners comfortable come rain or shine.

Why an Outdoor Kitchen?

Although there are plenty of good reasons to consider an outdoor kitchen, the decision must be based on your needs. Here are examples of why you might want to consider installing something beyond a basic grill:

- You grill at least twice a week during the warmer months and even have been known to fire the burners in the depths of a frigid winter.
- You're aching to try something beyond the usual burgers and boneless chicken breasts, but your equipment is not up to the job.
- You routinely find yourself cooking food indoors and bringing it out to the patio or deck for family meals or entertaining.
- You feel trapped in the house at the end of the day because you don't have pleasant outdoor living space.

If one or more of these descriptions fits you, an outdoor kitchen likely will be a worthwhile investment.

Like all investments, an outdoor kitchen requires an infusion of cash. You can find a solution that will fit into any reasonable budget, from under $1,000 for a very basic do-it-yourself setup of grill, work surfaces, and storage; to $2,500 for a weatherproof modular kitchen in stainless steel; to a $60,000 (or more) all-inclusive package with a commercial grill, stone counters, and an array of appliances—all nestled in a spacious pavilion.

Which raises one final question: Just what do you need to rightly call your space an "outdoor kitchen?" Although no single description works for everyone, the basic components are similar for all: a grill or other outdoor cooking equipment, some preparation space, and a dining area. Some outdoor kitchens go far beyond these basics to include fireplaces or fire pits, seating and gathering areas, multiple cooking and cleanup stations, and generous food storage capacity.

A fancy grill—or even a new grill—isn't necessary to create an outdoor kitchen. Convenience features such as ample counterspace, closed storage, and a separate side burner greatly enhance the outdoor cooking experience.

OUTDOOR KITCHENS BY THE NUMBERS

A 2006 study by Weber, an outdoor cooking equipment manufacturer, shows a rise in popularity and importance of outdoor rooms, which are defined as an "outside area with a cooking, eating, and sitting/entertaining place."
Here's what respondents' outdoor rooms contained:
- A grill and outdoor eating facilities: 97%
- Lighting: 48%
- Outside stereo systems or speakers: 42%
- Fireplaces: 32%
- Televisions: 15%

Respondents also said their outdoor room:
- Is at their primary home: 99%
- Is located in a suburb: 78%
- Is used for grilling: 59%
- 55% of those owning an outdoor room report "spending more time at home."

- 49% of respondents said that the design of their outdoor room was just as important as that of the rooms inside their home.
- 47% of respondents said the focus of their outdoor room is the grill, followed by the patio dining room set (45%) and a separate sitting or entertaining area (33%).
- 45% of respondents' free time between July and September was spent in their outdoor room.
- 44% of respondents who do not currently own an outdoor room said they are either "very interested" or "somewhat interested" in creating one.
- Respondents said their outdoor rooms comfortably accommodate an average of 18.4 people. The top three items they plan on including in their outdoor room are a grill (97%), a dining set (81%), and an outdoor fireplace (79%).

The Basic Outdoor Kitchen

An outdoor kitchen can be designed to prepare and serve food for a crowd of 200 or an intimate gathering of two. The major difference between these extremes is the capacity of the equipment and the size of the space. Both kitchens use the same basic elements:

Grill (or other cooking equipment). Although gas is more convenient and popular, charcoal proponents claim it offers unique flavor. Wood-fired ovens are a strong, relatively recent trend. Electricity is also an option.

Food prep area. A generous counter—at least 3 linear feet adjacent to the grill—is critical for preparing or staging anything more complicated than a plate of burgers. Adding a sink and refrigerator increases the convenience factor, but neither is as irreplaceable as counterspace.

Dining area. You can carry food inside, but most owners of outdoor kitchens would insist that having a comfortable and convenient place to eat outdoors is an essential element of the experience. A dinette set located on a firm, even surface—ideally sheltered from wind, sun, and rain—is the easiest way to add this capability. If you want an arrangement that encourages mingling with the cook, consider a dining bar built into the kitchen's counter.

Worthwhile add-ons. If you're a serious cook, think about adding a side burner. A rotisserie unit is popular for roasting whole birds and large cuts of meat. Remember to add light to your cooking center to enjoy your kitchen well into the short days of fall—and for late-night entertaining.

Already have a deck? An outdoor kitchen is a logical next step. It is a relatively simple task to build a countertop and grill support to create a kitchen; add other elements according to your budget and needs.

A small patio with a great view, a few container plants, a simple dining set—this minimalist outdoor kitchen covers the basics with style.

Types of Cooking

If unadorned grilling is your goal, about any grill will do. To set your sights a bit higher, explore the many types of cooking available with a well-equipped kitchen. Some of these optional cooking tools, like side burners, provide enough versatility to handle a wide variety of recipes. Others such as a pizza oven specialize in doing a handful of cooking chores very well. The options you choose depend both on budget and on the range of foods you expect to prepare. (The chart on page 21 matches cooking style with the foods to which they are best suited.)

Here's a look at the types of cooking you can do in a backyard setting. The specific equipment for handling each type will be examined later.

Grilling. Although often called "barbecuing," the vast majority of outdoor cooking is grilling. Food held above a heat source is being grilled. A grate keeps fat from accumulating under the food so that it is grilled rather than fried.

Grilling comes in two versions: direct and indirect. In direct grilling food is placed right above the heat source. This provides intense heat and fast cooking but can dry out larger cuts of meat that require longer cooking. With indirect grilling food is placed to the side of the heat source. The heat source warms the air and inner surfaces of the grill, which in turn cooks the food. Indirect grilling, which is actually closer to roasting, provides gentler heat, making it ideal for larger cuts of meat that require longer cooking times. Many expert grillers use indirect grilling exclusively.

Barbecue and smoking. True barbecue involves a long cooking period at a low temperature. Most barbecue is augmented with wood chips, which are soaked in water or other liquid, then heated until they smoke. This adds a distinctive flavor to the food. Different species of wood provide different flavor profiles. Smoking is similar, but with more smoke (and more smoke flavor). The long, low-temperature cooking process of barbecue and smoking breaks down connective tissue in the toughest cuts of meat, leaving them tender and moist.

An infrared burner mounted at the back of this grill is used with a rotisserie unit to evenly heat food.

This smoker holds food on racks in the upper chamber. The heat and smoke source is in compartments below.

Side burners allow using traditional cooking equipment such as saute pans, stockpots, and woks.

Because temperature control is critical and the cooking time is lengthy, barbecue and smoking require patience and regular attention. Some recipes call for dry rub, which means applying spices to the meat beforehand; others suggest regular applications of barbecue sauce.

Although ordinary grills can be pressed into service to barbecue, specialized equipment such as smokers or barbecue cookers, which provide separate chambers for food and fuel, produce the best results.

Side burner. A side burner is similar to a burner you'd find on a traditional gas stove, though many produce much more heat than a traditional indoor burner. Side burners allow using stovetop utensils such as sauce pans, stockpots, fryers, and woks. The high temperature is especially useful for bringing a large kettle of water to boil for corn or seafood. Lower temperature cooking methods—cooking with butter for example—can be a challenge for side burners that can't be turned to very low heat.

Rotisserie. In this cooking method, the food (usually meat or poultry) rotates as it is cooked at a low temperature. Many grills and barbecue cookers include fittings for installing an electrical rotisserie unit. The long,

slow cooking tenderizes the food, while the rotation allows the natural juices to coat the food rather than immediately drip away. Rotisserie cooking is ideal for large cuts of meat and whole poultry because it ensures even cooking on all sides. Both direct and indirect heat can be used in rotisserie cooking, and many newer grills now include special burners designed for this type of cooking.

Wood-fired ovens. If authentic pizza is your passion, you'll find nothing produces pizzeria-quality results like a wood-fired oven. These large masonry structures are designed to reach and hold very high temperatures. A steel or stone cooking surface guarantees rapid transfer of heat to the crust. In addition to turning out great pizzas, wood-fired ovens can be used for baking breads and roasting meats.

Open-fire cooking. Campers are familiar with roasting hot dogs over a campfire or cooking with a Dutch oven over a bed of hot coals. Though not especially difficult to master, open-fire cooking takes a bit of learning and patience to do well and is not within the repertoire of most outdoor kitchens. Fireplaces can be used for this type of cooking, as can fire pits. Both types of wood-burning amenities also offer the benefits of heat and light.

This grill has a narrow drawer that can be filled with wood chips, which are heated to produce smoke for barbecue flavor.

A fireplace is great for toasting marshmallows, providing a natural focal point, creating a romantic atmosphere, and warming chilly night air.

As you consider which cooking appliances to include in an outdoor kitchen, think about the types of food you like to prepare. This chart helps make the match. Accessories such as woks or skewers might be needed in some cases.

Type of Food	Grill	Barbecue/ Smoker	Rotisserie	Side Burner	Wood-Fired Oven	Open Fire
Burgers, hot dogs, boneless chicken, steak	✖			●		●
Roasts and large cuts of meat	●	✖	✖		✖	●
Whole poultry	●	✖	✖		✖	
Ribs	●	✖	✖		●	
Fish	✖	✖		●	●	✖
Shellfish	●	●		✖		
Vegetables	✖			✖		●
Sauces				✖		●
Stir-fries	●			✖		●
Pasta (boiled)				✖		●
Pasta (baked)	●				●	
Bread	●				✖	●
Pizza	●			●	✖	●

Cooking Appliance (●=possible; ✖=best)

This built-in wood-fired grill, oven, and smoker combines versatility with true wood-smoke flavor.

Five Key Functions

Planning an outdoor kitchen can be a daunting task. Hundreds of decisions must be made, ranging from the most basic—gas or charcoal—to the finer points of materials, location, amenities, and space allocation. Even the decision of whether to do it yourself or hire the work out can be complicated by budget realities, personal preferences, and available tools and skills. Designing an outdoor kitchen is every bit as challenging as designing an indoor kitchen, with the added consideration of rainfall, temperature swings, and changing light conditions.

To make the planning process easier, set aside decisions on very specific issues such as which grill to buy. Instead concentrate on your needs in five discrete areas: storage, food preparation, cooking, dining, and cleanup. Each must be accounted for in every outdoor kitchen plan. Ideally all will be integrated into the final project, although some of them may need to be relegated to inside the home.

This section addresses the issues and considerations affecting each of these functions. The next chapter explores options for bringing each one to life.

STORAGE

In indoor kitchens, cooks depend on having everything they need within a few steps. Pots, pans, and utensils often are tucked away in drawers or base cabinets that are within reach of the range. Staples and dry goods fill wall cabinets or a pantry just a few steps away. Perishable foods are kept at a safe temperature in a large refrigerator. The ideal outdoor kitchen also includes storage for equipment and food, though generally in smaller sizes than in regular kitchens.

Sometimes a little ingenuity goes a long way. Short on cold storage? A sink filled with ice can double as a beverage cooler, providing easy access to cold drinks without the expense of a separate refrigerator.

Include storage for bulky items such as charcoal bags and spare propane tanks.

Open storage can be decorative and functional. The lineup of hot sauces is within reach of the grill.

Dry storage is important for items that are staples in outdoor kitchens. Long-handled spatulas, frequently used cookware, serving platters and bowls, grill brushes, and cleaning supplies should be kept in closed storage to protect them from moisture and grime. All of these items should be close to the main cooking area.

If your climate is moderate, consider dry storage for nonperishable foods used frequently—spices and canned foods, for example. Bear in mind, however, that heat is an enemy of many foods, including ones that don't require refrigeration. Spices, for example, lose their potency much more quickly if exposed to high temperatures and sunlight.

You'll also need a place to keep bulky equipment—a spare propane tank or a portable side burner—used only occasionally. These items can be stored in a closed, safe, out-of-the-way spot.

Cold storage can be used to hold meat, poultry, or fish, or to keep beverages chilled. Perishable foods must be stored at temperatures under 40°F. Cold storage can be achieved with an undercounter refrigerator, a built-in ice bucket, or a separate ice chest. Whatever method you choose, monitor the temperature frequently. Raw or cooked meat and poultry spoils quickly, especially in summer's elevated temperatures.

Temporary storage can be a lifesaver if you entertain large groups only occasionally. Look for a rolling cart to augment storage capacity. This is a much more flexible arrangement than trying to plan a kitchen to handle every situation that arises. For temporary cold storage, consider a rolling ice chest, or fill a bucket or basin with ice and use it to dispense chilled drinks.

This cleanup zone includes a standard sink plumbed for hot and cold water with access to the supply lines and drain, provided here by stainless-steel doors.

FOOD PREPARATION

Next to cooking equipment, counterspace is critical to every outdoor kitchen. You'll need at least 3 feet of 24-inch wide counterspace adjacent to each cooking area. In addition to being weatherproof, a functional counter must be heat resistant and easy to clean.

If you have the room and the budget, install a sink with cold running water and a drain for washing produce or filling stockpots. If your budget is limited, purchase a modular unit that includes a sink, counter, and storage cabinet. Hook-up requires attaching a food-grade hose for water and a bucket to catch the drain water. A more permanent solution is a fully plumbed sink draining into your home's drain system or a dry well. In climates where temperatures drop below freezing, you'll need a way to drain the system to prevent burst pipes.

COOKING

Welcome to the main event. The heart of the outdoor kitchen is the grill. Traditionalists prefer the flavor imparted by charcoal, but it is hard to argue with the convenience of gas, especially a permanent natural gas hookup. Whichever choice you make, get a grill with the rack capacity, power, and accessories to handle the type of cooking you expect to do. Bear in mind that bigger isn't always better. Larger grills may offer much more surface area than you'll ever use, and will throw off plenty of heat. If two grills are the same price, the larger unit is likely to be less sturdy and more prone to wear and weather damage.

It's tempting to compare grills on the basis of cooking heat (expressed in BTUs), but that's not necessarily an indication of how evenly the heat is distributed or whether the lid does a good job of keeping the temperature even. Compare the shape and design of gas burners as well as their capacity. Talk to owners of grills similar to the ones you are considering, and read magazine and website reviews to get a handle on performance and convenience.

If you are considering adding other cooking appliances, ponder where they should be placed. A side burner should be close to the grill, but not immediately adjacent if possible. Smokers, fire pits, and wood-fired ovens are best located a bit away from the general flow of traffic so that their smoke and fumes don't irritate guests.

Decide whether you'll need a ventilation system. Some building codes require a vent hood if the outdoor kitchen is attached to the house. Powerful vent hoods are also desirable in windy climates.

Tile counters are ideal for prep zones because they are heat resistant, weatherproof, and easy to clean.

DINING

The amount of space allotted for the dining area depends on the type of meals you want to serve. For intimate family meals with two or four people, a 10×10-foot space is the minimum. For most homeowners, a 10×20-foot space is a better starting point. This provides you room for a patio table and chairs, while leaving ample space for some extra seating and traffic through the area.

Decks and patios can accommodate a table and chair set, but a patio is a better choice if you have the option. Chair legs can get caught easily in the gaps between deck boards. Decks also can become slippery when wet. A well-built patio provides a relatively smooth surface and should drain quickly after a hard rain.

In most climates a dining area benefits from provisions for shelter and privacy.

If you entertain regularly, size becomes critical in planning a dining area. Use graph paper and paper cutouts to represent the chairs, benches, and tables needed to accommodate the largest number of guests you expect. Include aisles at least 3 feet wide to avoid bottlenecks. Check that the paths from table to buffet to house are direct and easy to navigate.

If you don't have room for a table, or want something more conducive to conversations with the cook, include a snack bar near the cooking zone. Don't put the grill on the same counter as the snack bar, however, or you'll risk burning your visitors or enveloping them in smoke. It also makes sense to have the grill separated from the dining table for the same reason. The airborne heat, smoke, and moisture created by a grill are also good reasons to consider the prevailing breezes when you plan your kitchen: Keep dining and gathering areas upwind of the cooking station if you can.

A canvas roof held aloft by a metal frame and sheer drapes turn this deck dining area into a shady, private retreat.

CLEANUP

Although not the most glamorous aspect of a new kitchen, the cleanup function is still important. A well-appointed food prep area, especially one with hot water available, easily can do double-duty for cooking cleanup. You'll want a standard-size sink, not a small prep sink, to handwash dishes and utensils. A link to the home's drainage system is also important if the drain will carry greasy water.

Even without such niceties, you can ease the cleanup burden simply by making room for a trash receptacle and a recycling bin. Cover both to keep out animals and rain.

This simple horseshoe-shaped kitchen provides all the critical functions in one compact package.

Amenities

Beyond the five basic functional areas, other features deserve consideration when planning an outdoor kitchen. These amenities are not critical in every situation but provide benefits that may be desirable for your space.

Climate control. Fireplaces and fire pits, patio heaters, umbrellas, awnings, shelters, outdoor-rated fans, misting units, and even outdoor air conditioners moderate temperature swings throughout the year. If you live in an area with four distinct seasons, decide whether you'll use your kitchen in the off-season without help fighting off Mother Nature.

Privacy screens. Most of us prefer to choose when we are exposed to the world and when we'd rather enjoy our privacy. A private outdoor cooking and eating area can be achieved several ways. One way is to locate these areas so that the existing home or garage blocks views from outside.

Landscaping—trees, shrubs, and vines—can provide screening year-round or only during warmer months. Purpose-built privacy screens such as fences and walls can do the trick as well. Remember to consider privacy from above. An umbrella or pergola will block the view of your dinner table from nearby second-story windows.

Lighting. A well-designed lighting plan offers a lot of benefits at a very low price. Low-voltage systems are ideal for do-it-yourselfers and provide a broad range of fixture types. Choose spotlights for illuminating counters, floodlights for highlighting landscape features, and low-profile fixtures to brighten stairways. For an even easier installation, drape strings of party lights over railings or along counters. You even can purchase patio umbrellas with lights integrated into the frame.

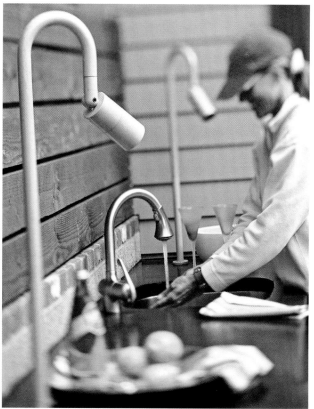

Elegant light fixtures brighten the prep area of this outdoor kitchen.

A gas-powered patio heater provides an island of warmth around the dinette set on chilly evenings.

A gathering spot in front of an outdoor fireplace offers a world of privacy and an infinite view. It's a combination of cozy and wide open that makes an ideal location for entertaining or relaxing.

2

Imagine the

With a basic overview of outdoor kitchen functions, amenities, and features, it's time to dream—to think about what a new outdoor kitchen will look like ... feel like ... be like. What materials will it be made from? How will it be laid out? What will it look like from the house and yard? Just as important, what view will it offer? Will it feature an expansive view, like the one shown here, or will it be a shady, more intimate spot? To help this chapter offers a gallery of great outdoor kitchens for your inspiration.

Possibilities

Ristorante Alfresco

Have a small yard with views you'd just as soon block out? An outdoor kitchen could be just the solution. Here a small backyard garden in a new development offered no privacy—and the view was mostly of neighboring houses' siding and windows. The homeowners love entertaining outdoors, so they turned the area into a private dining space that provides a sense of cozy enclosure while allowing them to enjoy the open air.

A gently arched brick structure gracefully envelops the area with separate niches for a built-in gas grill, a wine cellar and pouring area, and a fireplace that warms the courtyard on chilly evenings. The structure is open to the central eating and seating areas, allowing cooks to socialize with guests. A pergola provides filtered daylight, and the concrete floor—inlaid with brick—is dyed black and polished for a dramatic, high-luster, low-maintenance finish.

Lots of container plants landscape the courtyard-like space, preserving an outdoor feel. The dining set made of wrought iron and glass disappears against the black floor, showcasing the food and making it appear to hover temptingly in midair.

A faux-painted restaurant facade on the brick wall adds a sense of depth, light, and whimsy to this kitchen and was less costly than facing the wall with marble or tile. The arches shelter the cooking and wine-serving areas from weathering and provide a sense of enclosure.

Poolside Picnic

Who wants to leave the pool to come in for a meal? More and more pool owners and their families and guests are finding out they don't have to.

This pool area is an ideal gathering spot for family and social events, as well as a perfect play space for children, but it is located far from the indoor kitchen. Just fetching a cool drink on a hot day could result in a trail of wet footprints through the house. Provisions for outdoor meals would have to be ferried from one room to another before arriving at the terrace dining table.

Now a new Arts and Crafts-style addition shelters a compact, U-shape kitchen. On one side is a sink; on the other, a bar-sized refrigerator. A built-in charcoal grill does the cooking. The appliances are stainless steel for low maintenance and longevity. Granite counter surfaces top cabinets fabricated from marine plywood and finished with exterior-grade paint so the entire kitchen can be hosed clean. Underfoot, random-laid Hackett stone provides a subdued, natural look and firm footing. Channels cut in the stone drain water.

Rough-sawn square posts and brackets, exposed rafters, and hanging metal lanterns give this kitchen an Arts and Crafts feel that complements the house, a 1930s cottage. The low-pitched roof shades the cook while bathers take advantage of the sunny patio to warm up after a swim.

Plantings put a finishing touch on an outdoor kitchen. To soften the landscape pots of vinca, impatiens, dwarf conifers, and hibiscus surround the pool. Mandavilla tumbles from a balcony and English ivy and trumpet vines scramble up the walls.

This kitchen may have the architectural bones of a rustic park pavilion, but it is well equipped. Facing the entry is a charcoal grill set into a brick foundation (concealed by a granite face) for fire safety. Vents beneath the unit route smoke to a roof outlet, keeping smoke out of the cook's eyes.

The kitchen's metal lanterns are electrified, providing task and ambient lighting after the sun goes down. There's plenty of undercounter storage for cooking utensils, serving dishes, and table linens so supplies needn't be carted from the house. The countertop is extended along one edge for dining space and to accommodate buffets. A stainless-steel sink with garbage disposer speeds meal prep and cleanup.

In an outdoor kitchen, every element is a design element. This kitchen's rough stone piers do more than support the roof: They match the home's exterior wall and their robust proportions make room for deep countertops with plenty of space underneath for appliances and storage cabinets.

PLANNING FOR FOUR SEASONS

The warm southern states lead the trend in outdoor kitchens, but they are also popular in the Midwest and Northeast, says Mary Jo Peterson, a kitchen and bath designer in Brookfield, Connecticut. Peterson offers these tips for planning an outdoor kitchen in a four-season climate:

- Check that appliances and surfacing materials can tolerate repeated freeze-thaw cycles. If the grill will be left outside year-round, it should be constructed entirely of stainless steel (even cast aluminum will eventually pit and corrode).
- A roof that is just big enough may not be enough to keep rain-driven runoff from damaging appliances. Build one with an extended overhang or install gutters and downspouts to keep rainwater from accumulating inside the cooking area. If it's difficult to protect a refrigerator, for example, from snow and water, consider building a self-draining icebox.
- Make sure that the shelter doesn't block ventilation. Large grills—no matter their fuel—can generate a terrific amount of heat, so they need plenty of venting space.
- Put the grill where smoke won't drift into the house or drive guests off the deck or patio. Build chimneys for wood-fired ovens and fireplaces for the same reason unless they are well away from cooking areas.
- If possible keep the outdoor kitchen near the house—you'll be more likely to use it if you can retreat quickly inside when the weather turns.

Made in the Shade

This outdoor kitchen has it all—and then some! There's a stovetop, a gas grill with rotisserie, a warming drawer, a smoker, and a charcoal grill. They all add up to serious cooking capacity and the ability to generate too much heat to be exhausted from an indoor kitchen.

That's the reason for this raised-level brick-and-limestone pavilion in the garden. There's plenty of fresh air to waft heat, and two chimneys carry off the smoke. The formal, symmetrical design of the French-country-style pavilion suits the showmanship of the blooms and fountains in the formal garden surrounding it.

Although food preparation takes center stage, there's plenty of room inside for everything from intimate gatherings to huge catered dinner parties.

Each function has a separate area, cued in each case by a signature piece of architectural detailing: the range hood over the cooking area, the fireplace in the sitting area, and the dining table in the dining area. The three zones are unified by the whitewashed brick walls, which add texture while keeping the interior from feeling too dark.

The focal point of this seating and gathering area is a fireplace with a massive 16th-century sculpted-stone mantle. The fireplace is not just for decoration. It provides a welcome glow on chilly evenings and its shallow, tall build is custom-designed to use it for cooking as well.

A made-to-order, extra-long copper hood spans a suite of stainless equipment worthy of a barbeque gourmet. The hood vents heat, smoke, and cooking odors out two chimneys. Beneath it a reclaimed antique beam and a circa-1840s French burnished-steel butcher's hook rack extend the rustic charm.

Two chimneys hint at the many cooking functions of this garden pavilion. The structure's sense of age and character comes from its classic proportions, a green slate roof, and reclaimed building materials that include Louis XV stone balusters and a 19th-century dormer window made of cast iron.

Mahogany plank-front cabinets and a deep copper sink with oil-rubbed bronze fixtures occupy a niche near the pavilion's dining and lounging areas. Special undercounter amenities include a stainless-steel icemaker and refrigerator. The upper cabinet in this soaring pantry hides a large-screen television for after-dinner entertainment.

A carved marble dining table originating in 18th-century Italy defines the dining area. No matter what side of the table they're on, guests command views of the surrounding gardens and fountain. Elegant wrought-iron chairs complement the railing's graceful scrollwork.

Stone Wall Action

If you live in an area with abundant native stone, make the most of your bounty when building an outdoor kitchen. The material's timeless appeal and infinite life mean that it will be around for generations.

The mixed but mostly granite walls and structure of this woodland kitchen are appealingly rough and variegated. Its smooth, square slate patio tiles make a surface that is easily walkable. Plenty of plantings—small, well-placed trees, neatly-clipped shrubbery, and containers that can be moved about to fine-tune the look—soften and lighten the massive, quarried appearance.

The rock-solid feel of the stacked-stone walls demands outdoor furniture with equal presence. A wrought-iron dining set fills the bill perfectly. Its heft matches the

architecture, yet the delicate, tendril design mimics the plantings and ties together the two elements.

The result is an excellent example of why materials, landscaping, and furnishings are best considered as a whole when planning an outdoor kitchen. The reward is a coherent decorating theme, rather than a haphazard combination of materials and design elements.

A built-in stainless-steel grill is as impervious to the elements as the 2-inch-thick, stone countertop next to it. The cooking and seating areas are raised slightly, helping set them off from the central dining area.

Nothing creates the feeling of an outdoor room better—or gathers guests more quickly—than a fireplace. Even when it's not burning, a fireplace creates a natural focal point for a seating area.

Wrought-iron furniture is a great choice because its heft and texture ground it to the stone, while its delicate tracery blends with the plants. A bar-height table in a nook behind the seating area accommodates additional diners.

Sited at the foot of a green hillside, this kitchen turns what could be an unsightly concrete retaining wall into a design feature. Molded into the shape of a bench and stained to complement the adjoining stone wall and weathered roof supports, the sun-warmed seat is a favorite spot for bathers to soak up heat as they dry off after a dip.

Let the Sun Shine In

Pool, patio, pergola—who says you can't have it all? Massive overhead beams radiate from a fireplace to make this patio-corner kitchen the star of the yard. A whimsical, lattice-like tracery of a roof animates the area below with a constantly changing array of shadows as the sun courses the sky. The kitchen faces the shallow end of a pool, tempting bathers to ascend the steps and partake of goodies—from snacks to meals—prepared for them.

The construction of this kitchen is a reminder that pergolas, though originally designed to support climbing plants, are wonderful architectural elements. With or without greenery, they do a great job of enclosing an area while allowing light and air to enter. Unlike pavilions and cabanas, pergolas don't have walls that obscure views. Pergolas are also "adjustable." Want more shade? Plant some vines! Looking for a bit more sun in the seating area? Trim them back.

A diner's eye-view of the prep area reveals a kitchen that looks just as good from the inside as it does from the outside. Warm stone tiles contrast with cool stainless-steel appliances and cabinet doors.

Don't be fooled by the kitchen's lattice structure. Its half-walls of stone veneer house substantial amenities. There's a drop-in, hooded, stainless-steel gas grill with storage underneath, an undercounter refrigerator, a small prep sink, and lots of stone-topped counterspace that doubles as a snack bar. Carefully aimed spotlights hung from beams provide task illumination and ambiance after dark. There's even a sound system. Waterproof speakers—in white to complement the stucco fireplace surround—pump out the tunes.

Strong horizontal lines complement the design and scale of the ranch house served by this kitchen. Bathers find the rinse-off station on the post in the foreground a convenient and practical feature when it's time for a snack or meal; there's no need for soggy treks through the house to use the indoor shower.

The cooking corner is ideally placed to serve diners at both the counter near the food prep area and in the centrally located dining and gathering area. A mix of materials—stone, stucco, stained concrete, natural wood, even firebrick—offers a pleasing range of tones and textures.

Viva la Villa

Old-world ambience was the goal of this outdoor kitchen and pool area, and it succeeds brilliantly. The kitchen inhabits a roofed cabana overlooking a brick spa with a waterfall into a tranquil blue pool. A sunny patio for lounging edges the watery oasis; a stucco wall with weathered brick trim and arched, shuttered windows stylishly enclose the space.

The kitchen itself has all the amenities. A grill, refrigerator, and sink make the room perfect for weeknight family dinners. An icemaker, cooktop, and rotisserie ensure enough cooking capacity for a large crowd.

Food is served in an adjacent dining area reminiscent of a cozy European cafe, with weathered pillars and antique furniture. There's also a television and sound system in the cabana, making it a favorite spot for unwinding after work.

The view from inside was carefully planned to evoke a sense of peace and tranquility previously absent in this small yard in a developed neighborhood. The stucco wall, the statuary—even the banana trees planted at the property's perimeter—set a Mediterranean mood.

Slanting, late-afternoon sunlight warms an antique trestle table and bench in the cabana's dining area. The cabana floor is elevated slightly to allow the best view of the pool.

EUROPEAN EVOLUTION

If you have a home with European flavor, the ambience doesn't have to stop at the back door. Here's how this outdoor kitchen and pool keep continental influence flowing:

Transitions. The covered outdoor kitchen and seating area is open on two sides to the rest of the courtyard, making the most of outdoor views.

Scale. The yard is small, and a big pool would have overwhelmed the space and removed opportunities to add European-inspired detailing. The pool's custom shape, brick coping, and waterfall from the hot tub create a serene water feature that doesn't dominate.

Materials. Rough beams, rustic stucco, and weathered brick impart a feeling of age.

Decor. Antique furniture, including a wooden table and benches, lends to the cabana's old-world style. Antique shutters flank arched windows, and antique fencing stretches across the window openings.

Ambience. To match the old-world flavor that pairs buildings with canals, the pool is placed next to the cabana.

Cushioned wicker chairs, reclaimed beams, and used brick walls create an established, welcoming interior. A large gas grill is set into the stone countertops along with a powerful two-burner cooktop. New doors made from weathered wood give access to storage below.

Inside Out

Mixing materials and textures is part of the fun of designing an outdoor kitchen. So is the chance to work up an "interior" using "outside" materials. Since the entire area is exposed to weather, practical considerations are as urgent as aesthetics here. This kitchen artfully combines three types of stonework with stucco and wrought iron to create a cooking and entertaining space that's beautiful, durable, and functional.

A wet-laid, natural flagstone floor offers an even surface that's comfortable to stand on and easy to clean. Just sweep or hose it down periodically and powerwash it once a year. It will look like new season after season. The random shapes and smooth texture of the flagstones create interesting, abstract patterns that contrast with the pizza oven's rough, linear stone block enclosure. The crystalline sparkle of highly polished granite countertops offers stunning looks and wipe-clean convenience.

The kitchen's diverse elements are united by the muted browns, golds, and yellows of the three types of stone—tones supported by a creamy stucco wall and piers and a pergola that is milk chocolate brown. Botanical-inspired ironwork doors on the undercounter storage compartments and the trellis "backsplash" link the kitchen's solid structure with its lushly landscaped backdrop.

Weathered teak patio furniture and a stone bench equipped with comfortable cushions in awning stripes create a comfortable, casual seating area. Sheltering stucco walls and a crackling fire also add coziness.

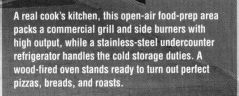

A real cook's kitchen, this open-air food-prep area packs a commercial grill and side burners with high output, while a stainless-steel undercounter refrigerator handles the cold storage duties. A wood-fired oven stands ready to turn out perfect pizzas, breads, and roasts.

Summer House

The traditional summer retreat is a cabin on the shore, but weekend traffic, maintenance hassles, and complex family schedules make many families think twice about owning one. Often a backyard retreat is a more practical option—and one that can be used and enjoyed far more.

This open pavilion is a case in point. The 21×31-foot structure turns the far end of a suburban family's pool into a full-featured vacation spot that's useable from early spring until well into autumn. There's a kitchen with bar seating for whipping up snacks to full meals, a television built into the cabinet for entertainment, and a small bathroom behind the kitchen.

A fireplace, sofa, and chairs furnish the other end of the space, offering a great spot for lounging, toasting marshmallows, and warming up after a swim. The fireplace sports distinctive sloping shoulders broad enough to block harsh wind and sun, but low enough to maintain the pavilion's open feel. There's no need to troop into the main house for anything.

This open, three-season kitchen design uses typical interior kitchen cabinetry despite the lack of walls and four-season climate. The secret: weatherproof folding doors that close to protect the cabinetry, appliances, and television from weather.

Family and friends can lounge on the sofa and chairs fireside after splashing in the pool. Arts and Crafts–style sconce lighting on the limestone chimney adds ambience when dusk falls.

The roofline and columns of this expansive cooking, dining, and gathering pavilion are designed to mimic the Arts and Crafts–style of the main house. Architectural harmony is an important consideration when adding a structure this large to an existing lot.

Because the main house is steps away, this outdoor kitchen focuses on the essentials: a built-in professional-grade grill with storage underneath flanked by deep prep surfaces. The massive granite base, hefty pavilion posts, and beefy purlins give this small kitchen big presence.

Small-Space Retreat

If you'd love a pavilion and a pool with an outdoor kitchen but are short on space, don't despair. Clever design, natural materials, thoughtful landscaping, and attention to detail can create a relaxing, full-featured outdoor environment without an estate-size expanse of ground.

Here's an example: This newly constructed house on a small, steep urban lot has no backyard—just a patio. Its owners created a private, spa-like spot.

The outdoor kitchen is nestled under a small pavilion disguised as an arbor. Although it appears open to the sky, it features a roof of laminated glass that keeps the grill and countertops—and the food prepared there—free from dust and debris from surrounding trees.

Just steps away a cast-aluminum dining set offers seating for four and hosts family dinners and get-togethers with close friends. The spa tub with its keyhole shape and comfy lounge chairs complete the space.

What's the secret to making a small space as satisfying as a big one? The answer lies in attention to quality and a design that makes the most of a site's assets. In this case high-quality masonry and a wonderful treetop location offer a great view and an infinite expanse of sky. The result is an open yet grounded feeling that's perfect for entertaining and intimate relaxation.

A magnolia tree and fence covered with vines provide privacy and soften the lines of the stone paving and granite wall. Lots of flowers in pots and containers add warmth and color.

La Casa de las Palmas

Named for the palms that surround it, this poolside outdoor kitchen in Southern California has the feel of a casual tropical resort. This favorite hangout and entertaining spot features handsome stone and wood structures, terrazzo-look concrete countertops, seating for fifteen, and a garden setting.

Flagstone floors and a wall of stacked flagstone unify this kitchen's interior, while providing durable, natural surfaces that withstand exposure and hard use. The cutouts in the wall were the homeowner's idea. After the walls were completed, she felt that the kitchen was dark and missed the opportunity to take in views of surrounding gardens. She punctuated the wall with handdrawn shapes in chalk and asked the contractors to cut them out and line them with flagstone frames. The accents took three weeks to execute, but they are what she envisioned.

The same attention to detail informed the concrete countertops poured on site. The contractor chose a granite aggregate and the homeowner selected several colors of pebbles. After pouring, the surface was ground, polished, and sealed. The result showcases the gemlike sparkle and varied tones of the mix, giving the countertops the look of terrazzo—and making them easy to clean.

A radiant heater mounted over the eating bar warms diners on cool evenings. There's even a firebowl built into the raised seating area in the rear for toasting marshmallows for s'mores.

Meticulously constructed of hand-selected stone—shimmed, in some cases, with stone slivers—this kitchen's surrounding wall offers a strong textural backdrop to its stone-impregnated, polished concrete countertops. The counters are deep enough for open beverage and glassware storage, adding convenience and visual interest.

Burlap-weave chairs, rush-and-bamboo placemats, and potted plants add texture and a tropical feel to the dining area.

To achieve two textures from the same material, the kitchen's lower surfaces—its floor and undercounter areas—are executed in smooth, natural-surface flagstone. The surrounding wall is made of stacked flagstone inset with cut granite to add texture and a geometric pattern. Gleaming stainless-steel appliances offer textural contrast as well as a low-maintenance finish.

Fully equipped with commercial appliances, this outdoor kitchen is designed for the serious cook. Amenities include, from left to right, a warming drawer, a drop-in, stainless-steel grill, a matching two-burner range, and refrigerator/icemaker. Custom-designed rock-ledge shelves hold hot sauces, a nod to this kitchen owner's love of spicy cooking.

With its perimeter clad in rock and rimmed with tropical plants, this shady kitchen offers a cool contrast to the sunny patio and pool. Custom-designed containers contribute artful shape—and the advantage of movable foliage.

Misty Glade

This combination kitchen and spa almost looks like a natural hot spring at the base of a moss-covered ledge. Yet the project was meticulously planned and executed in stages over the course of three years and fills a tiny backyard once dominated by the driveway to a garage—proof of how a visionary and well-executed outdoor kitchen project can transform an ordinary yard.

Key to including so much in such a small space is the integration of the kitchen and spa. The curving stone wall that nestles the spa pool also serves as the counter and backsplash of the food prep area—for large parties it triples as a bar.

It's the nature of that curving wall that gives the project its special character. The custom-quarried countertop is supported by a limestone wall with a footrest ledge for people sitting in the bar stools across from the cook. The wall sweeps under a waterfall and devolves into what looks like a natural, moss-covered ledge (in fact, the greenery cascading down the rocks is sedum, chosen for its ability to flourish in very little soil).

Natural flagstone paving contrasts in shape, color, and texture with the limestone. Flagstone also gives good traction even when wet—an important safety consideration near water.

An artfully constructed limestone wall follows the curvature of the spa pool. The pool's keyhole shape allows a stepped descent while keeping the pool's footprint to a minimum. Falling water masks street and mechanical noises.

What is more romantic than a shaded seating area with a view of the pool? An elaborate wrought-iron post lamp echoes the lines of the lawn furniture and provides evening illumination.

A change in levels marks the transition from the kitchen to the pool area. Layers of landscaping create nearly complete privacy in this small urban yard without requiring a hardscape fence.

Cupped behind a stone-topped barlike counter, the kitchen is located between the spa and the pool, affording a view of both. A wall-mounted lamp illuminates the food-prep area only, allowing for moodier lighting in the pool and patio areas.

Small but popular, this outdoor living area is used nearly every day. It also hosts family gatherings, cookouts, school parties, engagement parties, and philanthropic events. Its series of intimate spaces is an advantage, even with large groups. The spaces allow smaller groups to congregate without feeling lost, while large groups can move freely between the two areas.

Trellises planted with climbing vines add a vertical dimension to the landscaping and allow lush greenery to surround this outdoor living space. Most of the garden—including the containers—is automatically irrigated. Weekly visits from a professional gardener keep everything trim and healthy.

3

Comfort

Creating an environment in an outdoor kitchen that is comfortable, welcoming, and convenient for food preparation is a worthy goal. This chapter talks about creating that environment with the right combination of shelter, climate control, furnishings—even lighting options and sound equipment.

 # Shelter

In some climates shelter is necessary for an outdoor kitchen. In others it extends the season and allows a kitchen to be used in a wider variety of weather conditions. No matter where you live, it's worth considering how to keep a kitchen comfortable when visited by sun, wind, and rain. The range of options spans from nearly complete enclosure to wide-open exposure. Somewhere along that continuum is the right approach for your climate, site, and intended use. Here is a sampling of choices, ranging from elaborate to simple.

This kitchen is enclosed on two sides and tucked under a porch. High ceilings and a large window over the food preparation area maintain good ventilation and an outside feel. A canvas awning further shelters the kitchen and eating area, screening sunlight and offering protection from rain.

A dedicated kitchen structure provides for robust protection against the elements in a fully detached outdoor kitchen, above and right. This gazebo-style kitchen features a picturesque, steeply pitched roof with generous overhangs that keep the interior dry and pleasant even in a downpour. The enclosed sides face prevailing winds, and surrounding evergreens supplement the windbreak.

The pergola offers a great middle ground between enclosure and full exposure, especially for a semidetached kitchen and eating area. Here the pergola extends the protection offered by the main house's overhanging second floor. Substantial brick piers lend continuity and solidity. Robust overhead beams contribute to the feeling of security. They also screen the sun while allowing cooling breezes to enter—and smoke, heat, and cooking odors to escape.

This semipermanent roof, constructed of durable awning material, stretched over a metal frame shelters the kitchen from the elements and shades the cook.

Sun umbrellas are both practical and decorative for shading sitting areas and outdoor dining spots. These crank-up umbrellas are inexpensive, portable, and can be tilted to put shade where it's needed without obscuring a view. They're available as part of dining sets or as accessories that come with their own stands.

Besides hard structures, consider other solutions for shelter. For many climates and weather conditions, fabric shelters can offer adequate protection at substantially less cost. They also have a light, resortlike feel that instantly creates a summery mood. Some fabric structures can be retracted easily or taken down when not needed. Others are light-transmitting, filtering harsh glare but providing a pleasant, diffused glow that's easier on the eyes than full shade.

This awning and awning frame, readily available at home centers, make an attractive, functional, and relatively inexpensive shelter for a deck dining area. The translucent fabric provides shade, yet allows pleasantly diffused light.

A Pergola Primer

Good outdoor kitchens are designed to fend off the slings and arrows of extreme weather, but sheltering them still can be a good idea. Some luxury versions are enclosed in pavilions to protect pricey appliances, electronics, or wood cabinetry, but if your kitchen doesn't need that level of pampering, a pergola will provide some shelter much more affordably.

Pergolas are simple garden structures designed to provide shade while leaving their sides open for ventilation. At their simplest, pergolas consist of several posts tied with a set of beams called girders. The posts typically extend into the ground or are bolted to concrete pier footings, and the girders support joists (or purlins) and sometimes smaller boards that create gridwork overhead. They aren't rain-tight, but they block and/or filter sunlight. Their inviting atmosphere offers the psychological comfort of shelter without the literal enclosure. Pergolas are simple and affordable to build, and they retain views and sense of outdoor space.

The ancient original versions of these structures were intended as projecting roofs that provided shade at the perimeter of a home. It's still common to see pergolas attached to exterior walls to cover a deck or patio. Nowadays, however, many are freestanding and positioned to cover other landscape features such as poolside areas, detached decks, outdoor dining areas, and outdoor kitchens. Some support vines and other climbing plants to provide more shade or ornamentation. Unlike arbors, which they resemble, pergolas usually are larger and are intended as gathering areas that need to be furnished.

A poolside kitchen pergola serves several purposes. It acts as a backyard design focal point, defines the cooking and eating areas, and creates partial shade during hours of full sun.

A BASIC PERGOLA

Sturdy, handsome, and easy to build, pergolas are popular outdoor kitchen structures. Here are the parts that make the whole:

1. 6×6 (nominal) cedar or pressure-treated pine posts
2. 4×12 cedar girders (or double 2×12 stock)
3. 4×8 cedar purlins (or double 2×8 stock)
4. 2×2 lath
5. Pier footings should anchor at least two posts

DESIGN AND MATERIALS

Pergolas are frames rather than buildings, so they can't rely on finish materials to enhance the design. The components should be substantial enough to carry the structural loads and to convey the right visual weight. Here are the basic "ingredients" you'll need:

• **Posts.** Count on a minimum post size of 6×6 (nominal) for pergolas with a footprint up to around 150 square feet; for larger structures use 8×8 or larger posts.

• **Girders.** These beams connect the tops of the posts, and they are normally fitted around the perimeter of the structure. The overall size of the pergola will dictate the girder size; smaller structures can use 2-by lumber, typically 2×8 or 2×10 for modest spans. (Building codes specify these requirements, so ask local building officials for input.) For a heftier look and/or longer spans, use 4-by or thicker beams as required. You also can sandwich two or more 2-by boards to make a thick beam assembly.

Decorative shapes are easier to cut at beam ends because you can cut the boards individually with a jigsaw before assembly.

• **Purlins.** Lighter beams that rest upon the girders, purlins are closely spaced (usually within 2 feet of each other) and often at least one or two lumber sizes smaller than the girders. They connect the frame more solidly and provide a base for lath or other small boards to be attached above. In a pavilion or a conventional building, these would be the joists to which roof sheathing is attached.

• **Lath.** This refers to numerous narrow boards or square-profile strips attached to the purlins. Spaced with narrow gaps, they create a shifting pattern of sunlight and shade throughout the day or provide a base for climbing vines.

LUMBER SIZES: NOMINAL VS. ACTUAL

If you're new to building with wood, learn one quirky fact about how lumber is classified and sold. Hardwoods for furniture and cabinetry often are sold by specialty retailers, and the boards are typically random widths and lengths. Only the thickness is consistent and is described in quarters of an inch (4/4, 6/4, and so on). The thickness is nominal (in name only), because milling the lumber smooth removes some material and creates a thinner board. This also is true for softwoods and the dimensioned lumber typically used for building projects, although the naming system uses different labels (1-by, 2-by, and so on). A 2×4 comes from the sawmill roughly that size (in inches); after milling and drying it will actually measure 1.5×3.5 inches. Lumber designated as "1-by" material is actually ¾-inch thick. Other lumber sizes are similarly reduced from their nominal designation, so make sure your project designs and plans reflect the actual dimensions.

This pergola was designed to define the dining area. Combined with the fireplace and chimney, it distinguishes the dining area from the bar area (to the left) and the sunbathing area (to the right).

POST ANCHORING

Pergolas are top-heavy structures, so anchoring the posts securely in the ground is critical. Under most circumstances the posts should extend below grade in a heavy concrete pier footing. As a general rule, at least 25 percent of the post length should be in the ground. If the frost line for your region is deeper than that, use it as your guide.

On our project example, the existing patio slab and the proximity of the pool prevented the use of pier footings for two of the posts, so they are anchored with metal post base hardware. The remaining two posts are anchored deep in pier footings in order to stabilize the pergola frame. (See illustrations, page 75.)

POST OPTIONS AND DECORATIVE DETAILS

Here's a closer look at how the pergola can be anchored and how to create the decorative detailing on the girder and purlin ends.

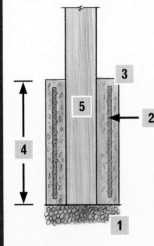

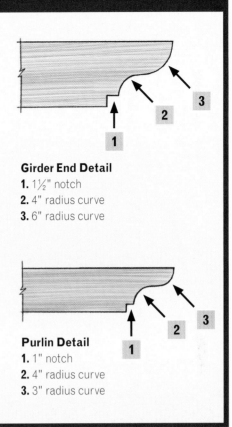

Girder End Detail
1. 1½" notch
2. 4" radius curve
3. 6" radius curve

Post Option 1
1. Crushed rock
2. Steel rebar
3. Concrete pier footing
4. Minimum 25 percent post inground or to frost depth
5. 6×6 post

Post Option 2
1. Existing slab
2. Anchor bolts
3. Stand-off metal bracket for post base
4. 6×6 post

Purlin Detail
1. 1" notch
2. 4" radius curve
3. 3" radius curve

Twin pergolas shelter and define separate seating and dining areas in this poolside retreat.

Pergolas are adaptable to different building styles. Classical columns give the pergola a formal air that complements this pavilion to which it's attached.

Privacy Trellis

While you might not be concerned about absolute privacy, most people want to enjoy an outdoor kitchen without being on display. Lattice panels, grid trellises, and woven fence designs can buffer adjoining yards without cutting off breezes or outbound views.

DESIGN AND MATERIALS

Ready-made lattice panels are readily available. You also can realize a more customized look with patterns of your own design. Making trellis panels requires a table saw, pneumatic stapler, and other specialty tools that any qualified carpenter owns. You can stick with stock lumber sizes; using unusual spacing or arrangements provides the custom look.

Western red cedar is ideal for such projects. It's easily accessible, reasonably inexpensive, lightweight, workable, and resistant to rot and insect damage.

The trellis panels shown here feature two sizes of narrow cedar boards—1 inch wide and 2¾ inches wide. Grouping them creatively and using the pattern both vertically and horizontally creates a woven effect. For making more than a few panels, build a jig to space the parts automatically for nailing. If you're not doing volume work, at least make a story pole—a guide board marked to show where the slats and gaps belong.

Use stainless-steel staples or finish nails; they help prevent the discoloration and staining that ordinary fasteners produce when used in cedar.

THINK OUTSIDE THE "BOXWOOD"

Because wood is such a great material for trellis panels and privacy screens, it is easy to forget there are alternatives. Products that can weave a fashion statement are: manufactured vinyl lattice screens, copper pipe, perforated metal sheets, wire mesh, hardware cloth, or braided metal cable.

An arrangement of two different widths of cedar boards gives this privacy panel a custom, woven look. Lightweight, naturally rot-resistant, and easy to work with, cedar is an ideal material for such projects.

A PRIVACY SCREEN

This screen achieves a custom look with stock lumber—all grid stock is 1-by cedar, and 4×4 posts and 2×4 cap rails means you can skip the resawing and move right on to building.

1. All grid stock is 1-by cedar
   -1" wide narrow strips
   -2¾" wide strips
   (see detail on grid spacing)
2. 1" wide frame stiles
3. 4×4 post
4. 1" wide frame rails
5. 2×4 rail cap
6. Post final

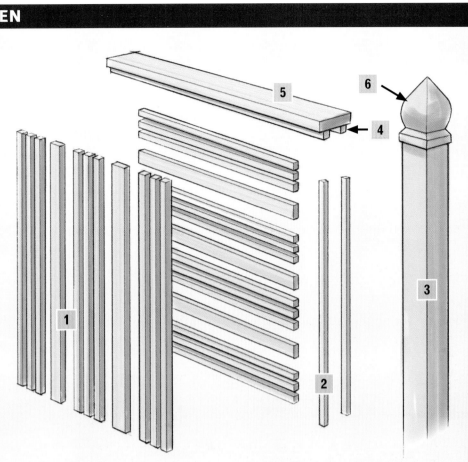

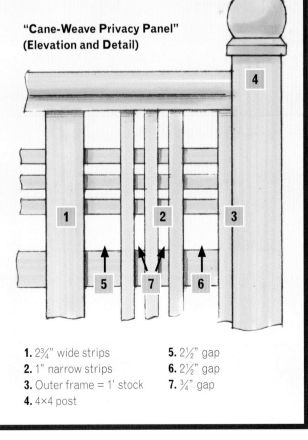

"Cane-Weave Privacy Panel"
(Elevation and Detail)

1. 2¾" wide strips
2. 1" narrow strips
3. Outer frame = 1' stock
4. 4×4 post
5. 2½" gap
6. 2½" gap
7. ¾" gap

Temperature Control

Comfortable generally implies "temperate." Here are strategies for keeping hot and cold extremes at bay.

COOLING

Providing shade and locating your project to take advantage of prevailing breezes is often enough to keep an outdoor kitchen comfortable. If those precautions aren't sufficient, stir up relief with a fan. Ceiling-mounted units are naturals for covered areas—they're quiet and unobtrusive and cool a comparatively large area. Freestanding fans—including those equipped with misting units that add cooling moisture to the moving air—are other options. In hot, dry climates, permanently installed misting systems can cool the air to a surprising degree. If cost is no object, you even can install outdoor air-conditioning units that pump cool air from strategically located vents. Such units work well only in dead calm conditions and only in a contained area.

WARMTH

Adding warmth—both visual warmth and the kind you can feel—can be a priority because outdoor kitchens often are used in the evenings or at night when temperatures are lowest. Outdoor kitchen owners are also eager to use them in the spring and reluctant to abandon them in the fall. Adding a fireplace is a preferred choice for many reasons. In addition to providing heat and light, fireplaces perfume the area with the aroma of burning wood, create a natural gathering spot, and inspire a "campfire" atmosphere that encourages marshmallow toasting, s'more making, and storytelling. Fire pits—both those permanently built into the ground and portable units made of sheet metal—are other popular options that afford 360-degree seating and don't require an expensive, view-restricting chimney. And electric and gas appliances can turn up the heat as well.

Even traditional arrangements of hearths and chimneys can be creative. This fireplace embellished and rimmed with tile adds shape and color to an outdoor dining area, radiating charm even when it's not burning. The elevated hearth invites guests to sit by the fire.

A semienclosed outdoor kitchen with a barrel-vaulted ceiling is ideal for a ceiling fan. Diners and cook alike benefit from its cooling effect.

No room or budget for a masonry, but still want a traditional fireplace? Consider a clay chiminea. With origins in South and Central America and enjoying recent popularity everywhere, chimineas can be situated almost anywhere—even on a deck where a masonry unit would be too heavy.

This fireplace forgoes a typical chimney structure—its sweeping shape combined with prevailing winds create a vacuum that sucks smoke up and out. The concave wall also focuses the fire's heat into the seating area and provides a windbreak.

Fire pits—essentially fireplaces without chimneys—have advantages. They're open on all sides so they radiate light and heat evenly throughout their surroundings, allowing large groups to gather 'round. You can build a permanent fire pit for a fraction of the cost of a fireplace (see page 81) or you can buy a portable metal unit such as this one, which can also function as a grill.

Building an Inground Fire Pit

Indoor fireplaces rank high on the list of features people want. These fixtures are more about ambience than function, as few people rely on them as a heat source. Still the appeal of fire remains, and it translates to outdoor environments.

Even if you do your outdoor cooking on a gas grill, a fire pit can provide a focal point for gathering before and after meals. It also can extend the season for your outdoor kitchen by providing lots of radiant heat in cooler climates.

If you live in a rural area, your options are likely plentiful. Many urban areas prohibit open outdoor fires for safety and air quality reasons, but fire pits used for cooking often are exempted from these rules. Call city or county offices and check the local regulations.

You can build or buy a freestanding fire pit to use above ground. Made of metal or masonry, many are portable and feature a cooking grate and/or a spark screen.

Building a fire pit below grade, however, has advantages. The fire is sheltered from the wind, so it tends to burn slower and longer, making ash less likely to become airborne.

If lining the pit with rock or masonry as shown in the illustrations, the extra thermal mass will absorb and release heat more evenly. The result is a steadier, modulated warmth rather than the erratic hot-and-cold cycles that occur with normal flare-ups and die-downs. If possible, site your fire pit so prevailing breezes will blow the smoke away from dining and cooking areas. Also avoid locations under trees where sparks could ignite overhead foliage.

For campfire ambience in your own backyard, a fire pit is just the ticket. Offering light, warmth, and 360-degree seating, fire pits are great for gathering, marshmallow-toasting, and conversation—and are relatively inexpensive and easy to build.

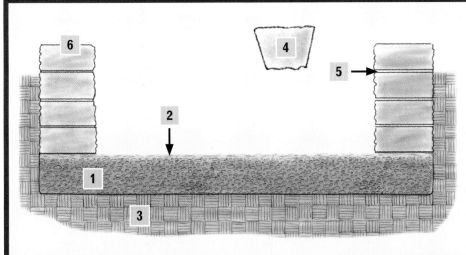

INGROUND FIRE PIT

In-ground, masonry fire pits require more labor than expertise. The materials and skills involved are simple:
1. 6" layer of crushed rock
2. Coarse sand fill in/over rock
3. Undisturbed soil
4. Modular concrete retaining-wall block with tapered sides (top view shown)
5. Concrete adhesive between courses
6. 1+ block stacked above grade

DESIGN AND MATERIALS

This fire pit is designed for wood burning and takes shape in a hole about 5 feet across and 18 inches deep. (For a gas-fueled fire pit, see Plumbing the Depths, below.) For a circular shape, use a wood stake and rope to make a simple compass. Use it to trace an outline on the ground. Remove the soil and check that the bottom of the hole is reasonably level, then fill it about 6 inches deep with gravel or crushed rock. Tamp the rock down firmly, then add sand and repeat. Most of the sand will filter down to fill voids in the rock; keep adding until you have a top layer of only sand, about 1 inch thick. This will provide a good setting base for ring blocks and also will make it easier to rake and scoop out ashes.

Modular concrete retaining wall blocks are ideal for a fire pit liner. Their uniform thickness makes stacking easier, the tapered shapes easily form a circular ring, and they are widely available and affordable. Buy enough for the liner ring to extend at least a full block above the surrounding grade; the added visibility will increase safety, and can help prevent pets and toddlers from accidentally tumbling over the edge.

Set the first course of block into a complete ring to check the fit, then use a rubber mallet to tamp each block firmly into the sand. Check for level then add the remaining courses. Use dabs of mortar or concrete adhesive between courses for stability.

If you need a cooking grate, contract with a local metalworking shop to weld one for you. While you're at it, see if they also can fabricate a cover for the pit to enclose it when it's not in use.

Building a large fire pit is relatively inexpensive using masonry landscaping blocks. Set the blocks on a gravel pad, tamp them in with a rubber mallet, and level them with a carpenter's level.

PLUMBING THE DEPTHS

If used to the convenience of a gas grill and a gas indoor fireplace, you may want the same feature in a fire pit. You'll need an accessible gas line and a professional plumber to make the connections. For as little as $100, you can find manufactured kits complete with burner rings and valve assembly, but the hookup should be handled by an experienced installer. Depending on your local climate and codes, the gas line may have to be buried below frost depth like a water line. This procedure likely will involve pulling a building permit, so check with local building officials before starting.

Furniture

Every outdoor room needs to be furnished. High-quality outdoor furniture options abound and come in three main types—wood, metal, and wicker.

WOOD

Wood furniture fits your style if you love natural things. The best-quality wood furniture is made from center cuts of lumber, the most dense and durable part of a tree. Low-grade or young lumber has a more inconsistent grain and color and should be less expensive. Look for furniture built with zinc-plated or stainless-steel screws and glue. The screws can be tightened if they loosen. Less expensive furniture uses riveted or stapled joints, which are more likely to fail and harder to repair.

Not all wood is created equal. Here's how different types stack up:

Cedar and pine are lightly colored, straight-grain softwoods. Pine rots quickly, but pressure-treated pine and cedar last many years. For maximum protection paint or seal either type of furniture.

Teak, one of the best wood performers for outdoor furniture, also is among the priciest. Harvested from plantations in tropical countries, teak possesses a stable, honey-colored grain and resists rot and decay. Even when exposed to the elements year-round, teak furniture lasts at least 50 years. Untreated teak fades to a silvery gray. To maintain the original color of the wood, apply teak oil to it once or twice a year.

Roble and jarrah, both hardwoods with delicious reddish tones, are relative newcomers to outdoor furniture. They're both rot-resistant; jarrah lasts up to 50 years, and roble, 25 years. Apply teak oil, boiled linseed oil, or marine oil to roble to preserve the wood's warm tones. Use a treatment specially designed for jarrah to preserve its natural color.

Painted pine outdoor furniture is classic, comfortable, and easy to move. It's best stored under cover when the season's over and requires periodic painting to look its best.

Teak furniture is a poolside favorite because splashes and wet towels won't harm it. The furniture is so durable it even can be left outdoors uncovered all year long.

Teak is extremely durable, and left unfinished weathers to a pleasant silvery grey color. Among the lowest-maintenance of all woods, it requires no sealing or staining to maintain its weather-resistance.

This custom-made, oiled-teak bench is simple but elegant. Its shape conforms to the gently curving edge of the deck and railing on which it sits.

These handsome teak chairs feature a classic modern style and vintage-look fabric cushions. Although the printed design is reminiscent of mid-century cotton covers, it is a synthetic material that's much more durable than its natural cousin.

OUTDOOR FABRICS

Unlike natural fibers such as cotton, acrylic fabrics endure outdoor conditions. You'll find two dramatically different acrylics on the market: solution-dyed acrylic and print (yarn-dyed) acrylic.

Solution-dyed acrylic contains UV-resistant pigments that are added to the acrylic in its initial liquid form. As a result fade-resistant color and easy cleanability are inherent in the fibers before they are even woven into fabric.

Yarn-dyed or print fabrics are woven first, then receive dyes or pigments on the fabric surface. This process allows more design possibilities than solution-dying. It sacrifices performance for style because print fabrics can fade.

How long should you expect outdoor fabric to last? Wearability varies depending on the manufacturer, but you can expect 1 to 3 years if the fabrics are properly maintained. Many manufacturers offer a warranty against fading and degradation of furniture.

Wrought-iron furniture combines grace, durability, and heft, as the fiddlehead detailing on this chair arm shows. A slight rust patina adds to its variegated finish.

METAL

Metal, one of the best-selling materials for outdoor furniture, is prized for its durability, comfort, and versatility. Two primary types of metal furniture are wrought iron and aluminum.

Wrought-iron furniture dates to the Victorian Era and still graces outdoor settings. Renowned for its ornate curves and traditional presence, wrought iron is both beloved and cursed for its considerable heft. Its weight makes it the most suitable furniture for windy sites. Many manufacturers now use finishes that protect against weathering. Cushions soften the hard seats and add a splash of color to the frames, which are usually finished in white, black, or green. Expect to pay more for intricate pieces, because much detailing is done by hand.

Aluminum furniture is either extruded or cast. Extruded-aluminum furniture frames are tubular and usually feature strap or sling seats. Their light weight makes the pieces easy to move, and their simple frame designs often make them suitable for stacking.

Cast aluminum offers more intricate design options and tends to weigh more, although it's still far lighter than wrought iron. Cast-aluminum frames often feature arm scrolls, interwoven backs, or embedded textures such as a bamboo pattern. Cast aluminum also may support contemporary slings and plush, deep cushions.

Thanks to powder-coated finishes, both types of aluminum come in a rainbow of hues and require little maintenance.

Extruded-aluminum outdoor dining sets often feature flowing lines and cool, comfortable fabrics. They also are lightweight—making them easy to reposition and store—and easy to maintain.

WICKER

Wicker and all-weather wicker possess the same woven look but are very different products.

Wicker furniture, most commonly woven from rattan vine, also can be made from cane or bamboo. The furniture pops up in a multitude of hues due to acrylic resin coloring during the manufacturing process. It is also available painted. Wicker's natural fibers make it unsuitable for exposed sites so it should be used outdoors only under a covered area such as a porch.

All-weather wicker, or outdoor wicker as it is sometimes called, mimics the classic look of traditional wicker. All-weather wicker is made from twisted paper or synthetic fibers woven around a frame coated with a weather-resistant finish. Both fade- and water-resistant, all-weather wicker stands up to the elements and poolside use although most manufacturers recommend that the furniture be protected from prolonged exposure to full sun.

All-weather wicker is widely available. Specialty stores offer many more fabric selections for cushions and more design options than big-box stores but with a higher price tag to match. Higher end stores sell all-weather wicker pieces paired with materials such as teak for a sophisticated look suitable for indoors or out.

Wraparound comfort and classic good looks characterize wicker furniture, which has been an icon of summer ease for more than a century.

Synthetic all-weather wicker withstands direct exposure to sun and rain better than natural wicker and is available in many fade-resistant colors. Because the material is often woven around a tubular steel frame, it's sturdy, and heavier than authentic wicker made of rattan and bamboo.

Natural wicker is made from woven rattan or cane fibers, often around a bamboo or wood frame. The furniture's open weave is decorative and offers natural ventilation, so it's cool and comfortable in hot weather. Natural wicker is available unfinished, dyed, or painted.

STONE FURNITURE

Natural stone, long a favorite material for walls, paving, countertops, chimneys, and other outdoor kitchen structural functions, is showing up as furniture. Of course! It's supremely durable, sculpturally beautiful, solid as a … well, you get the idea. Of all the furnishings in an outdoor kitchen, perhaps only stone pieces will not be blown over, rot, fade, rust, or crush when a tree limb breaks and falls on them. Don't expect to order stone furniture from a catalog. Many custom stone fabricators are creating their own pieces. A final note: Make sure these pieces are exactly where you want them before the installer leaves!

Two massive, squared boulders and a flat slab form an outdoor table with presence. The top's natural variegated color and texture give it character.

 # Lighting

Most outdoor kitchen owners continue cooking after the sun goes down. So plan on building sufficient illumination to make your kitchen safe, functional, and welcoming.

A well-designed lighting system illuminates cooking and food preparation areas, dining areas, seating and gathering areas, walkways and paths, pool surrounds, and stairs. Outdoor lighting fixtures also can help decorate an outdoor kitchen by highlighting plants, trees, and architectural elements such as walls and fireplaces. Security lighting addresses safety around foundation plantings and perimeter fences.

When planning a lighting scheme, keep the design flexible. Use several circuits and include dimmer switches to vary the amount of light in individual areas. Place switches indoors or under cover or use weatherproof switches rated for outdoor use. To avoid annoying glare, hide bulbs from direct view using shades, covers, or plantings. You also can direct the light to bounce off large reflective surfaces, such as walls.

Several types of lighting draw attention to the beverage center of this outdoor kitchen. Can lights overhead in the trellis provide lighting that is bright but not glaring for the countertop. An electrified lantern offers overall illumination. Candles placed in glass chimneys add mood and sparkle.

OUTDOOR LIGHTING CHOICES

Explore your alternatives when lighting an outdoor kitchen and surrounds. Possibilities range from traditional, building-mounted lights to low-voltage, solar, string outdoor lighting, and purpose-designed task lighting.

Wrought-iron brackets

Vintage-look pole lighting

Downlighting

Decorative string lights

Grill lights

Solar-powered accent lights

A wrought-iron bracket, hand-blown, bubbly-glass lenses and bulbs shaped like candle flames ensure that a wall sconce (top left) adds atmosphere as well as ambient light to a patio dining area.

Low-voltage lighting offers safe, economical outdoor lighting. Such systems support a range of fixture types that can be used for path, safety, decorative, or ambient lighting. Placing post lamp fixtures above raised beds, stairways, and other obstacles is good safety practice as well as an attractive addition to an outdoor room.

Incorporate perimeter lighting into your scheme. Building lamps into a surrounding fence or wall (top right) shows off these architectural elements at night and provides guests with a sense of enclosure and security.

Decorative string lights (bottom left) are available in a wide variety of designs and configurations. Although primarily designed to add sparkle and mood, they also can be used to outline pergolas, arbors, rooflines, posts, and piers, guiding cooks and diners around the kitchen's layout.

Also remember task lighting. Food preparation and safety require bright illumination. Concentrate it with gooseneck fixtures (bottom middle). Their focused beams are useful for conversation areas.

Get creative! Solar-powered outdoor accent lamps mounted on stakes are great to have around to illuminate everything from a pathway to the pool to an ice bucket (bottom right). Just stick them where you need them—no need to run wiring or install switches.

Landscape Lighting

It's easy to let big decisions about grills and garden furniture take precedence, but good lighting is just as essential for an outdoor kitchen. Landscape lighting is the quintessential multitasker: It improves the aesthetics of a landscape, makes a yard more usable, and enhances safety.

If you have a refrigerator or other electrical appliances, tie in the lines for outdoor task or ambient lighting. For the kitchen structure itself, standard lighting fixtures might be best, but better options (low-voltage and solar) are available for the surrounding landscape.

Include lighting decisions in the earliest planning stages, with fixtures and focal points indicated on a site map. Mark work zones that need task lighting, traffic paths that require safety lighting, and garden elements where you want to highlight the view or set a mood. In daylight a garden is what it is, but nightfall brings opportunity to shape what to spotlight (literally) and what is better relegated to shadows.

Take advantage of a variety of light sources to ensure that your outdoor living areas are well and attractively lit. Here, light spilling through French doors supplements a hanging fixture, decorative string lights, and strategically placed candles to create a warm ambience.

DESIGN AND MATERIALS

Low-voltage lighting systems are proven performers for outdoor use and are easily the most popular choices. These systems feature a transformer that plugs into a standard 120-volt electrical outlet. This converts the current to a safe 12-volt level that makes the fixtures better for outdoor use and easier to install. For areas where running cables is not practical, newer generations of solar light fixtures provide good illumination. (See Going Wireless, page 92.)

The transformer is the heart of the low-voltage system, and it will be rated (in watts) for the maximum electrical load it is designed to carry. A single unit can supply multiple circuits or fixtures, but the cumulative total of the lamp ratings should not exceed the transformer's rating. Most manufacturers offer kits with the right mix of transformer and lamps. Simply plug the transformer into an outlet and run the cables to the fixtures. (Unlike standard line-voltage wiring that has to be buried up to 24 inches deep, low-voltage cable is safe enough to leave at ground level. Camouflage it with mulch or groundcover.) If you purchase components piecemeal, make sure the transformer and cables can handle the total wattage load from all the lamps combined.

The right combination of safety, task, and accent lighting can keep your kitchen cooking after dark—and add to its visual appeal.

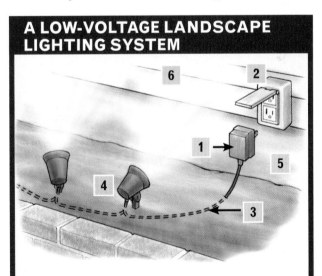

A LOW-VOLTAGE LANDSCAPE LIGHTING SYSTEM

Whether you buy it in kit form or assemble the pieces yourself, here's what you'll need to do to install a low-voltage lighting system:

1. Transformer (rated for amps to match fixture load)
2. GFCI outdoor receptacle in shielded housing
3. Buried low-voltage cable in mulch or ground cover
4. Low-voltage halogen or LED fixtures
5. Foundation wall
6. Siding

This tiki-torch path light is lit by the sun. Solar-powered landscape lights are easy to install—just stick them in the ground where you want them.

GOING WIRELESS: SOLAR FIXTURES ARE GROWING UP

If raw lighting power is the objective, industrial line-voltage fixtures will do. Most landscapes are better served with low levels of illumination, and solar fixtures make that easier than ever to achieve. With improvements in photovoltaic cells and LED lamps, today's solar lights have outputs far superior and longer lasting than the anemic versions offered when they first appeared on the consumer market. They couldn't be easier to use. Fasten them to a surface or press the mounting stake into the ground. They require careful placement for optimal exposure to sun, but some versions have remote solar panels tethered to the lamp fixture with a small cable that offer more flexibility; you can place the fixture where you want the light and the solar panel where it will get the most sun.

Early generation low-voltage systems used small incandescent bulbs, then came halogen lamps. Now they are more likely to feature LED (light-emitting diode) lamps. These solid-state lamps are extremely efficient at turning low levels of electricity into usable light, are immune to most impacts and cold temperatures, and have a life span that can reach 50,000 hours. They even can produce colored light.

Fixture designs are also evolving. Spot-, flood-, up- and downlights are available, along with decorative "rope" lights, stake-mounted path lighting, and colored accent lighting. Finishes and materials now include copper, stainless-steel, dark bronze, or faux housings that mimic rocks and other natural objects. Many transformers feature timers, motion sensors, or light sensors that can turn lights on or off on a regular schedule, whenever movement is detected, or at dusk and dawn.

Every landscape warrants an individualized lighting design, but all should feature the basics: downlighting for safety at steps and walkways, uplighting to highlight trees and architectural elements, washlighting to cast shadows on background surfaces, and a mix of intensity levels to emphasize some areas. Overlighting a landscape is a common mistake. Dim the intensity in areas that benefit from mood lighting.

Some low-voltage lighting is purely ornamental. This electrified, wound-wire dragonfly winks at evening guests from the foliage. It is one of a string of such accents cleverly placed throughout the surrounding plantings.

Pay attention to water features when planning an outdoor kitchen's lighting scheme. Illuminating pools, spas, and waterfalls adds ambience and safety.

A SOLAR LANDSCAPE LIGHTING SYSTEM

Option A: Self-contained LED fixtures

This option requires no wires or connections. Simply stick the fixtures in the ground and you're set.

1. Photovoltaic cell built into top of fixture housing
2. LED lamp
3. Walking path

Option B: Remote collector

This system allows locating the solar collector in a different place than the light, permitting solar lighting even in shady areas.

1. Remote photovoltaic cell attached via cable; placement for optimal sun exposure
2. LED spotlight placed near/under a plant or tree

 # Sound

Liven the gathering at your outdoor scene with quality speakers made to play in open air. Today's weatherproof outdoor speakers are designed to be mounted on the eaves of your house, an arbor, or a pergola. Some outdoor speakers can be hidden among plants in a pot, while others are the pot. You even can find convincing fake rocks that pump out great sound. At least one manufacturer will tint your "rock speakers" to match the real boulders in a landscape.

The difference between indoor and outdoor speakers is more than meets the eye. While even mild weather will destroy poorly protected indoor speakers, a high-quality outdoor speaker is designed to take everything Mother Nature dishes out—from heat and cold to rain and snow to ocean salt spray. Most manufacturers offer warranties that cover weather-related failures.

Outdoor speakers also differ from an acoustic standpoint. That's why if you drag your indoor speakers outside, you won't be as satisfied with their performance as you would if you were listening in your living room. Inside your house, the walls reflect and enhance sound. Few walls exist outside, and the landscape soaks up high and low frequencies, especially bass. To bring a fuller sound to your outdoor kitchen, audio engineers take such factors into account.

Outdoor speakers can be mounted permanently on exterior walls, concealed in ceiling structures, or positioned on pergolas.

This frog speaker adds whimsy and good sound to an outdoor setting. You can set it right on the ground and leave it there year-round without worry.

Some outdoor speakers can have conventional packaging. Simply place them in plain view and enjoy the music.

Outdoor speakers are designed to be weather resistant and acoustically tuned to an outdoor environment. This one is designed to radiate sound in all directions, compensating for the lack of a traditional room arrangement.

Speakers camouflaged as small boulders are yet another option for sound. Some can even be tinted to match local stone varieties or your garden's color scheme.

This flowerpot is a speaker! Connected with conventional speaker wire hidden in the undergrowth, it carries a tune without revealing its location. Wireless speaker options are also available.

4

Equip Your

The number and variety of accessories available to stock an outdoor kitchen is delightful—and perhaps overwhelming. Moving past grills are side burners, smokers, wood-fired ovens, refrigerators and other appliances, sinks, and other plumbing fixtures. This chapter is designed to review all the options. No matter the space or budget, there has never been a greater choice in outdoor cooking accessories than right now.

Outdoor Kitchen

 # Grills

In most outdoor kitchens, the grill is the most expensive single item. Purchasing one can be daunting because of the many features and technologies manufacturers offer. Most popular are gas grills, which come in a spectrum of price ranges and capabilities. Some purists opt for charcoal—a fuel choice that also offers various grill types and prices. Still others like wood-fired cooking: Pizza ovens, especially, are a rising trend. Here's a rundown of some of the choices:

If you grill at least once a week, often entertain crowds, and cook everything from chili to lobster outside, you're a gourmet griller. Only professional-grade materials and a grill with all the extras will do.

You'll pay a premium for one of these fancy machines. They are mates for life, with commercial-grade construction and warranties to match. Some are installed in an outdoor kitchen island or countertop; others are on wheels to move around as suits the cooking and entertaining situation.

In this category expect burners, flavor plates, grill grate, lid, and cart to glisten with heavy-gauge, high-quality stainless steel. One or both sides of the grill will have burners that can accommodate optional griddles. Trivets slip on for cooking with a wok or large stockpot. Love smoky-flavored food? You'll appreciate the smoking drawers and boxes on these grills.

Another standard feature: a heating device that uses intense infrared radiation instead of flames. The high heat quickly sears the outside of food, trapping tender juices inside. Sealed rotisseries keep hot air and flavor-generating vapors under the hood where they can permeate the food.

GOURMET GRILL EXTRAS

Gourmet grills boast plenty of extras. Super-hot infrared burners seal in flavor. Smoke boxes and sealed rotisseries help trap flavors under the hood. A large stainless-steel cooking grate provides enough grilling space to feed a crowd, cleans easily, and offers ample storage underneath. Knobs, handles, and other hardware have a high-quality feel.

Smoking tray

Sealed rotisserie

Infrared burner

Towel bar

Quality hardware

Stainless-steel grate

Storage

Grill light

The highest quality gourmet grills are loaded with extras. Popular features include rotisseries, enclosed storage, foldup prep areas, side burners, and stainless grates.

Base for a Built-In Gas Grill

Charcoal and gas grills belong front and center in an outdoor kitchen, and custom installations often feature a built-in rather than portable grilling unit. Traditionally, most grills were built into fireproof masonry bases made of brick or stone (see the Basic Grill Island on page 105) because the cooking heat wasn't well contained. Today's gas grills, however, concentrate heat upward toward the grates, and their metal housings often have internal insulation that keeps the outer surfaces cooler, making them safe for installation in wood enclosures. (This isn't true for every grill unit, so check the manufacturer's recommendations before taking this route.)

If the required clearances can be met, combustible materials such as wood can make design and construction of a grill station much more user friendly. Gone are the fixed modular sizes of bricks and blocks. Any size grill or side burner can be accommodated, by using cement backerboard topped with stucco or tile.

Building a grill—and perhaps a side burner—into a countertop brings the amenities of a commercial kitchen to your backyard. Abundant counter space, a backsplash, and ample storage are included. Insulated grills make possible a wider choice of construction materials.

A WOODFRAMED GRILL BASE

Wood construction is an alternative to masonry for an insulated grill. The project will include these elements:

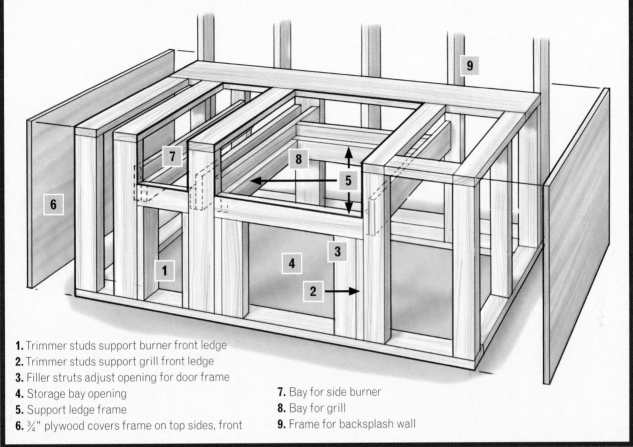

1. Trimmer studs support burner front ledge
2. Trimmer studs support grill front ledge
3. Filler struts adjust opening for door frame
4. Storage bay opening
5. Support ledge frame
6. ¾" plywood covers frame on top sides, front
7. Bay for side burner
8. Bay for grill
9. Frame for backsplash wall

DESIGN AND MATERIALS

Every outdoor grill designed for built-in use comes with an installation guide that outlines the specifications, clearances, and materials necessary for safe operation. Look for this information first, and plan your grill base accordingly.

If you can meet the manufacturer's recommendations with a woodframe structure, use pressure-treated pine lumber for the main parts of the frame. This material is durable, rot- and insect-resistant, inexpensive, and made for use outdoors.

Common sizes of 2-by framing lumber are required to produce the frame shown above. Heavy reinforcing or layering of stock creates support ledges for the appliances. This not only carries the grill's weight, but it adds rigidity to the frame. That stiffness helps prevent flexing that might crack an exterior masonry "skin" such as stucco or thin brick veneer.

Normally the support surfaces adjacent to the grill or burner housing are covered with a noncombustible shield of some sort. Cement backerboard, designed for use under ceramic and stone tiles, is ideal. It is easily cut and fastened, and corner joints can be taped and mortared.

Exterior-grade plywood sheathing can be used to cover and reinforce the outer frame of the base. That should be covered with roofing felt (tar paper) or a similar moisture barrier. Metal screen lath, nailed or screwed in place, is a substrate for the stucco finish.

WORKING WITH PRESSURE-TREATED LUMBER

Misinformation about the dangers of pressure-treated lumber can dissuade you from using this versatile and durable material. Most of the scare came from early-generation chemical treatments that contained small amounts of arsenic. Newer formulas do without that toxin, but have a higher percentage of copper, which tends to corrode ordinary steel fasteners. Use only hot-dipped galvanized or stainless-steel fasteners with treated lumber. Follow the precautions that make sense with any wood: wear a dust mask to avoid breathing fine particles and wash your hands after handling the material.

Even midpriced grills offer lots of function—and even a bit of flash—for the dollar. Expect at least stainless-steel accents and gratings, along with some enclosed storage, food prep surfaces, and perhaps a side burner.

Avid Grillers

If you cook outside year-round and prize a perfectly seared steak, you're probably an avid griller. Before buying, research grills with storage, built-in prep spaces, and high-heat burners.

These grills cost a bit less than gourmet grills, but still scream quality in look and performance, thanks to heavy-duty materials inside and outside. The grill lid should have double walls to contain the hot air and keep out drafts. If you give the unit a shake, you should hear few rattles, and its wheels should operate smoothly.

Grills in this category generally feature stainless-steel burners and flavor plates. All or part of the exterior body may be stainless steel as well. Be sure the stainless steel is at least grade 304.

Grill carts in this category typically have doors and backs to keep grilling utensils neatly hidden. Flip-up prep areas, towel bars, and shelves are other common perks. Cooking space may be as much as 700 square inches, and at least one side burner is standard.

LOOK FOR THESE FEATURES

The quality of these grills is noticeably better than entry-level units made for casual grillers. Look for a solid cart with locking wheels, an enclosed storage area, and a sturdy, practical grilling platform. Extras may include a towel bar or tool hangers. Flip-up prep surfaces and at least one side burner are standard. The cooking area should be somewhat larger than on lower-priced units, and perhaps made of stainless steel.

Locking wheels

Tool hangers

Side burners

Ample cooking area

A Basic Grill Island

The built-in barbecue grill evolved into the modern outdoor kitchen. Long before there were undercounter refrigerators, backyard rotisseries, and beverage centers that rivaled well-stocked bars, simple charcoal or propane grills fitted into brick or masonry surrounds. Some versions sported only a metal cooking grid over a brick-lined firebox; on others a stone slab provided some counterspace.

This simple installation still forms the core of an outdoor kitchen—no matter how many other amenities make their way into a project. The grill island provides three outdoor kitchen fundamentals: a powerful heat source, a prep surface for setting out food and dishes, and enclosed storage for accessories. If time or budget prohibit an extravagant outdoor kitchen, you still can start with this basic setup, then add to it as circumstances allow.

A grill island, dining set, and patio are all that's needed for a basic outdoor kitchen. Owning a patio and table and chairs means the picture is nearly complete.

A BASIC GRILL ISLAND

A grill island is a simple project, requiring readily available materials and modest construction skills. Here's how it goes together:

1. Concrete slab base (minimum 4" thick)
2. 4" wide concrete block
3. 8" wide concrete block to create rear ledge for grill support
4. Embedded angle-iron lintel to support opening for storage bay
5. Steel rebar (optional)
6. Gas line with valve (optional)
7. Tool mortar joints flat
8. Stucco scratch coat
9. Stucco finish coat

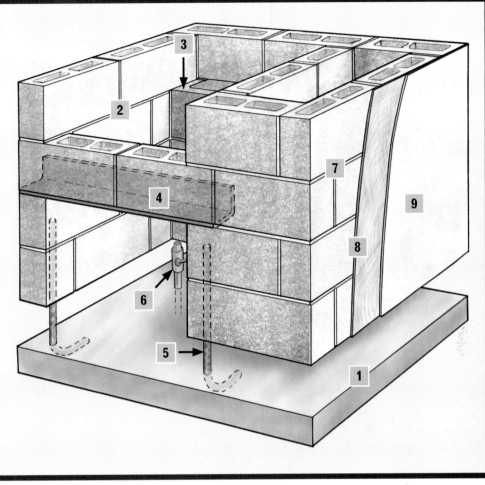

DESIGN AND MATERIALS

A grill station functions like an indoor kitchen cabinet with a cooktop—with important differences. It has to contain a more powerful heat source so combustible materials must be adequately protected or, when possible, omitted from the design. It has to withstand rain, wind, harsh sunlight, and in some areas, snow and freezing temperatures. Given these requirements, a conventional wood cabinet doesn't make sense for an exposed freestanding grill station.

You can mimic the construction of a building with a structural framework of wood covered with noncombustible and/or weatherproof materials, but this often adds more expense and another layer or two of work. Better to stay with materials that offer the properties you want, which translates to masonry.

Brick and natural stone have proven themselves for centuries, but they often involve higher costs and more skill. To keep things simple and affordable, a compact grill station can be built with modular gray concrete block, then covered with a decorative stucco finish. Or use decorative concrete block that doesn't require any finishing.

If this type of design and construction suits your project site and tastes, ensure the grill and other components fit properly and are adequately supported. Here are basics to consider:

• Install a concrete slab foundation first. The structure needs a stable base, and concrete is ideal for this. The slab should be at least 4 inches thick and rest on undisturbed soil or compacted fill material (crushed limestone is sometimes used as a subbase material for drainage and stability). Wire reinforcing mesh placed during pouring will help control cracking and separation of the slab; steel rebar can be embedded so it extends upward into the block bays. If you want a gas or water supply line inside the base, it must run underground and come up through the slab. This usually requires a permit, inspection, and specialized tools and skills, so have a licensed contractor add these features.

• Purchase the grill and any other built-in components (storage doors, a side burner, and so on) before finalizing the plans; build around their dimensions.

• Size the structure to use full modules of the block to

minimize cutting. The most common block size is 16 inches long, allowing for the mortar joint. You'll also find widths of 4, 6, and 8 inches readily available. Factor these widths into the overall dimensions, because they interlock at the corners. The version shown features 4-inch block for most of the side walls, but several courses of 8-inch block along the rear wall create a support ledge

for the back of the grill. This is simpler and more effective than attaching a wood cleat to the inside of the wall after the base is built.

• Open areas such as the storage door bay often require support above from a lintel, which is typically a piece of L-shape steel (called angle iron) that helps support the weight of the blocks above the opening.

TILE COUNTERTOP FOR A BASIC GRILL ISLAND

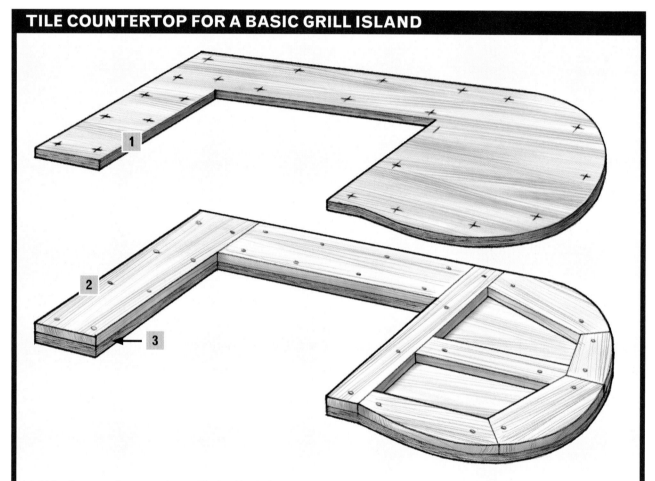

Add food preparation space to a grill island by building a tile countertop. Here's what is needed to build the plywood "sandwich" that supports the tile surface:

1. ¾" plywood top panel
2. 1× cedar or P.T. pine stock
3. Lower panel ¾" plywood

The tile countertop on this grill station is an ideal counterpart to the masonry and stucco base. It's simple, inexpensive, and can stand up to weather. The cantilevered design provides extra surface area without requiring a larger base, but it does mean the subassembly has to be strong and rigid. Like other masonry components, ceramic tile doesn't flex. If it's not supported uniformly it can break. Our version uses a layered construction of plywood and solid wood to create a thick and rigid, but relatively lightweight assembly:

• Use ¾" exterior-grade plywood for the upper and lower

panels as shown. Cut the first panel and use it as a template to mark and cut the other.

• Attach 1-by cedar or pressure-treated pine lumber as a center core between the plywood panels. Leave some small areas open, as shown on the circular portion of the cantilevered end.

• Use deck screws and exterior-grade wood glue to bond the subassembly. Use screws with masonry anchors to attach L-shape mounting brackets to the block base structure, then attach the countertop assembly with screws driven from below.

• Protect the plywood with a layer of felt underlayment (roofing or tar paper), then fasten a layer of cement backerboard for the tile base. Bed the tiles in thinset mortar; use tiles rated for exterior use so they don't absorb moisture and crack. Fill joints with grout and apply an exterior sealer. (For more on tile countertops, see pages 166-167.)

A tile countertop adds utility to a small island by providing extra work and serving space.

Casual Grillers

If you're more interested in basic functions than a load of options, you may do fine with one of these models. Even at entry-level prices, you'll discover a range of features and quality.

Grills at this end of the price range provide an average cooking surface area of 500 to 600 square inches, enough room to cook a big turkey or a bevy of burgers. The cooking grid and burners may be constructed from any of several materials, but even more important than the material (because many come with a limited lifetime warranty) is the design. For example, lower-end models may have L-shape or strip burners; H- or U-shape burners spread heat more evenly. Experts say one U-shape burner is as effective as two strip burners, and that even heat distribution is just as important as having a lot of burners.

At this price range look for quality construction and materials rather than lots of features. Food prep areas, a concealed gas bottle, and a temperature gauge are often standard.

This modestly priced grill offers an L-shape work space, foldup prep surface, temperature gauge, side burner, grease tray, and wire storage rack. The enameled steel lid is available in a variety of colors and is durable, although the manufacturer recommends covering the grill when it is not in use.

FEATURES

For better cooking results, look for a grill with a built-in thermometer. Without one, it's difficult to know the temperature of the cooking box. Carts support the grills but typically offer minimal storage. A single side burner, side that flips up, or fixed preparation space may complete the grill, but the price tag generally reflects an investment in the cooking unit rather than additional gadgets. Stainless-steel flourishes may appear on grills in this price range but may be more stylish than practical. The cooking area will be adequate for a family meal, but larger crowds will demand more food than these grills can deliver.

Multiple burners

Prep surfaces

Built-in thermometers

Features to Expect

Here are some materials and features to look for in a new gas grill.

STAINLESS STEEL

Stainless steel has been appearing recently on lower-priced grills. That's good news if you like the metal's gleam, but you usually get what you pay for. The quality of stainless steel is determined by its grade, not merely its thickness. For grills, grade 304 is considered good. If the quality is lower, the metal may corrode. Use a magnet to perform a simple test; if the stainless steel is grade 304 or better, the magnet won't stick. (It will stick to lower-quality steel.)

A TANK GAUGE OR CONCEALED TANK

When firing up a gas grill, the options are a propane tank or a natural gas line extended from your home. Both provide fast, efficient cooking. If you use natural gas indoors, running a line outdoors is usually a simple task any plumber can perform. The benefit? A constant, on-demand supply of gas. If you like to move your grill around your outdoor kitchen, you'll want the portability of propane. Look for a grill with a built-in tank gauge to avoid unexpectedly running out of cooking fuel. You also can have a large propane tank permanently installed for the best of both options.

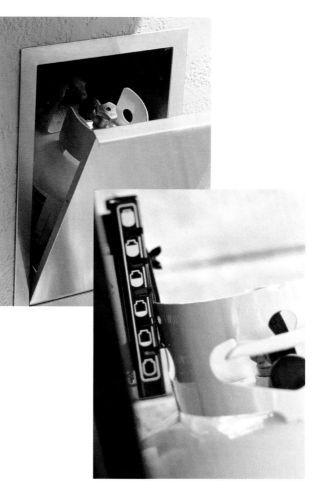

The grill's fuel tank is an often overlooked element. Ideally it will be equipped with a gauge to indicate how much gas is left, it will be concealed from view, and it will be easy to access. Having a spare, full tank on hand is a good idea as well.

Stainless-steel construction is the hallmark of commercial-grade kitchen appliances and high-end grills. Good grade stainless is virtually impervious to water damage and will look great for years. Stainless is also important in less visible areas such as fasteners and burners, so open the grill hood and look around before buying.

A match and a prayer are no way to light a gas grill. Push-button ignitors are safer and more convenient. The best are shielded from cooking spatter, which can render them inoperative.

Grease is the bane of the grill. Uncontained, it can turn the inside of a grill into a sludgy mess—and drip onto your deck or patio, staining it. Removable grease trays are elegant solutions.

A SHIELDED IGNITOR

You know the drill. You buy a new gas grill and the ignitor button works like a charm. Two months later you're striking a match, tossing it into the grill, and hoping you come away with both eyebrows. To take the singe out of outdoor cooking, purchase a grill with a protected ignitor button. When you're shopping peek inside the grill. If you can easily reach the exposed ignitor unit, grease and food juices can too. If you can't see it, the igniter is probably shielded inside a small box called a gas catcher, and the ignitor (and you) should enjoy a long, healthy life.

A REMOVABLE GREASE TRAY

Tired of that greasy tin can hanging from the bottom of the grill? Look for a grill with a removable, built-in grease tray. Juices that aren't burned up fall into the tray, which can be removed and tossed into the dishwasher. Grills at the lowest price levels don't usually have removable grease trays, but they're conveniences worth the price to avoid your deck or patio surface looking like the floor of a greasy-spoon eatery.

Alternatives to Gas

Considering that humans have been cooking food over wood and charcoal fires since prehistoric times, gas grills are fairly recent innovations. Many people prefer grilling, cooking, smoking, and baking with wood or charcoal for fuel—whether for the smoky taste, the even heat, or the simple nostalgia of cooking outdoors the way it's always been done.

If you're drawn to a solid-fuel fire, you'll be pleased to know that options from basic to gourmet are available. Here's a rundown.

THE CHARCOAL GOURMET

High-end charcoal-fired cookers combine sound engineering and commercial-grade materials with the most basic of heat sources. The result is a multipurpose appliance that is grill, smoker, and oven in one.

Some brands feature an adjustable firebox that can be raised and lowered to change cooking temperatures. A grease drain system keeps flare-ups to a minimum, and an internal heat-deflector plate turns the grill into a smoker. Dual draft vents enable control of the fire. A full-width fire door allows adding fuel while food is cooking—a function that's awkward with traditional charcoal grills.

Oven units can bake anything from pizza to bread as well as grill and smoke. Many have a range of accessories—rotisseries to rib racks—like some of the best gas grills.

THE MODERN ICON

The classic kettle grill has been updated in recent years with new features that include locking casters, tool holders, and weather-protected charcoal storage. Some even offer a gas charcoal-lighting system that eliminates the need for electric or chemical starters. Some models come with a food preparation surface and accessories that turn it into a pizza oven.

Now you can find a grill with the sleek stainless look of a modern gas unit—complete with wheeled cabinet, under-grill enclosed storage, and dual food preparation areas—that burns old-fashioned, aromatic charcoal. A crank raises and lowers the fire to control grilling temperature, the hood holds in heat, smoke and flavor, and an external thermometer monitors the internal temperature so you don't have to open the grill.

The portable charcoal grill has grown up recently, acquiring a gas-fired charcoal ignitor, prep surface, built-in charcoal storage bin, and a larger, more stable cart for easy transport.

The versatile design of a top-quality charcoal cooker allows it to serve as a grill, a smoker, or an oven.

CERAMIC COOKERS

Another recent spin on an age-old design is winning a new following. Ceramic and other egg-style cookers grill, smoke, and bake based on a 3000-year-old Asian cooker. Today's models are made out of space-age ceramics. Draft vents allow the cookers to start quickly and precisely maintain temperatures from 150 degrees up to 800 degrees. The interior material absorbs and radiates heat evenly, and the lid ensures that smoke, moisture, and flavor stay inside to permeate the food. Ceramic cookers also work as a grill or an oven, producing crisp pizzas and brick-oven crust breads. Gas-fired models are also available.

The insulated body of ceramic egg-type cookers greatly reduces temperatures on the outside of the cooker, even to the point that it can be built into a wooden cart.

Air vents at the top and bottom of egg-style cookers allow adjustment of airflow for precise temperature control. The damper door at the bottom permits ash removal. The lid seals tightly and the refractory materials inside retain heat evenly for quick cooking times.

Ceramic plus stainless steel plus charcoal plus two gas side burners in this model produce a cooking center that does it all. It also includes a removable porcelain grate with a non-stick surface for easy cleaning.

Expand your grilling repertoire well beyond burgers with a cast-iron skillet on the rack of a covered grill. A charcoal fire in this masonry fireplace provides the high heat needed for stir-fry recipes.

A slightly domed circle of sheet steel forms the cooking surface for this home-made Mongolian grill. The firebox is fashioned from a 55-gallon drum and filled with a combination of charcoal and wood for fuel.

Who says you need a grill for an outdoor kitchen? You can't get much more basic than this: a cast-iron pot over the open flame of a fire pit. This simple setting, however, can produce tasty stews, coblers, and much more.

Wood-Fired Ovens

Pizza gourmets say there is nothing like wood-fired ovens because they combine roasting, baking, and smoking to produce flavorful, evenly cooked food.

These ovens can prepare fish, poultry, pork, lamb, focaccia, and other breads—even tarts and pies. You can bake, roast, and (with the addition of a freestanding cast-iron grate) grill in a wood-fired oven.

Wood-fired ovens have other advantages. Their gentle radiant heat, dancing flames, and aromatic wood smoke infuse a kitchen with a delightful ambience. If you're considering putting a fireplace in your outdoor kitchen, think about taking the extra step of making it a wood-fired oven as well.

Although it's the wood fire that provides heat, the oven does the cooking. The secret of the great taste it can produce is exceptionally long-lasting, even heat. To bake, you fire the empty oven and let the special masonry refractory material come up to temperature. Then rake out the hot coals, brush out the oven, and use the heat retained in the oven's dome and floor to cook the food.

Depending on the heat generated by the fire and the type of cooking being done, you often can cook several batches of food with a single firing.

You also can roast, sear meat, or brown vegetables or bake casseroles in wood-fired ovens. Moving pans around the inside of the oven allows you to vary cooking temperatures. Add small pieces of wood to keep the oven producing the heat required.

Although most wood-fired ovens look custom-built, only the part you see is crafted on site. The oven behind the facade is generally mass produced, either as a modular oven that is factory made, then put together on site, or as a preassembled oven ready for enclosure. Enclosures are traditionally faced with brick, stone, or stucco. Because the ovens are placed at torso height to make cooking easier, there's often room for wood storage underneath.

Wood-fired ovens are traditionally installed so that the hearth is about 45 inches off the ground for no-stoop cooking. The space beneath the hearth is great for wood storage.

Wood-fired ovens are best known for their great-tasting pizzas, but they also excel at baking bread and pies and roasting and grilling meats.

Cooking Accessories

In addition to the abundance of primary cooking appliances available, a plethora of ancillary equipment can make your outdoor kitchen more versatile and well equipped than an indoor kitchen. Just about every item can be purchased as a separate unit, so you either can add items in stages as a budget allows or buy just what you need to accommodate your cooking and entertaining needs. Here's an overview of some of the products available.

BEVERAGE CENTERS

For built-in beverage service, this drop-in stainless-steel unit features a built-in sink, covered ice container, bottle storage, bottle opener, and towel hanger. Designed to be incorporated into an outdoor countertop or island, many beverage centers are built to restaurant standards.

INFRARED BURNERS

Infrared burners heat up faster and cook at higher temperatures, sealing in juices and flavor. Some grills have infrared burners built-in; other units stand alone or drop into a countertop and are available in a variety of sizes.

BEVERAGE CARTS

These rolling centers hold everything needed for quenching thirst when entertaining outdoors. This cart of wood and stainless steel combines storage with a pouring and serving surface. A sliding shelf system below holds dinnerware and napkins.

BLENDERS

What's a bar without a blender? Built-in units combine stainless construction with sliding covers and weatherproofed electrics. Stainless blender shelves with covered GFCI-equipped 120 volt electrical outlets add portability. The shelf functions equally well as a coffee-making center.

PIZZA OVENS

To add pizza-cooking capacity to an outdoor kitchen without building a wood-fired oven, purchase a pizza cart. It is a pizza oven on wheels that is gas-fired. Another version drops into a counter.

PREP CARTS

Experienced cooks know counterspace is at a premium. This prep cart combines a large cutting block with dual flip-up work areas, built-in vegetable trays, generous storage drawers and cabinets, and a towel hanger. The versatile, movable unit also can serve as a bar or buffet when food-prep duties are over.

SIDE BURNERS

Grills are great but they can't cook everything. For more conventional steaming, frying, and general heating, a gas-fired burner or two can come in handy. These drop-in tops are available with every feature of a commercial cooktop—including electronic ignition and high-capacity burners—and are built to resist the weather.

WARMING DRAWERS

These versatile units are designed specifically for keeping food warm or hot or for heating serving and eating dishes. They're available both as undercounter units or are built into some high-end cart-mounted cooking centers.

WOK BURNERS

It's hard to beat a wok for stir-fried perfection, but regular flat burners aren't configured to hold these round-bottomed pieces of cookware. Wok burners are specially designed side burners—often sold with a custom wok—that solve that problem. The burners come in a range of sizes and outputs.

REFRIGERATORS

Why troop inside for cold storage? Ideal for remote or freestanding island kitchens, outdoor-rated refrigerators offer stainless-steel good looks and weather resistance, and are sized to fit neatly beneath a countertop or island.

SMOKERS

While foods may be smoked in many outdoor grills, sometimes the required long cooking times and relatively low temperatures conflict with other grilling needs. A dedicated smoker is an ideal solution. Available in charcoal, gas, and electric models, smokers generally offer precise temperature control, upper and lower vents, and a vertical design that offers plenty of room to smoke large turkeys and roasts.

COOKING UTENSILS

You'll need utensils to clean your grill, baste, handle, and in some cases hold food while cooking the rest. Avoid short-handled utensils designed for stovetop cooking. They're a sure route to burned hands and dropped food. Invest in some of the following tools. You may not need all of them—let food preferences and cooking style be your guide.

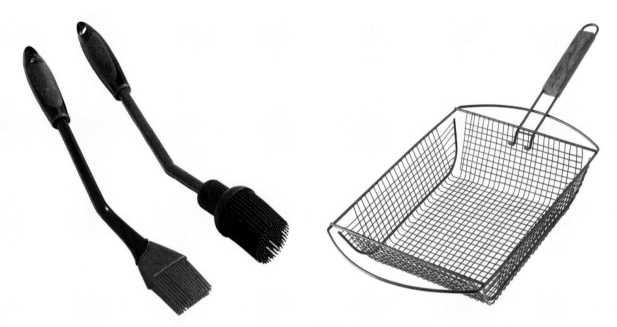

Silicone brushes are used for oiling the rack before grilling and brushing sauces and marinades over food and are easier to clean than old-fashioned natural fiber brushes.

Grilling baskets hold small or delicate foods such as fish, shrimp, or vegetables while grilling. Food can be stirred or shaken for even cooking. Some baskets are open; others have hinged lids.

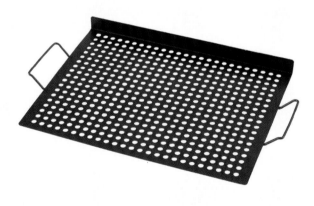

Grilling trays with a non-stick enamel coating allow heat and smoke to penetrate foods such as pizzas and diced foods that require more support than a grill grate can provide. They come in all shapes and sizes with and without raised edges and handles to accommodate a variety of grills and foods.

Kabob racks are built into some grills but they're available as universal accessories that rest on top of grilling racks. They allow cooking and turning kabobs easily, without risking food sticking to grill racks. Some accessory racks are equipped with stay-cool handles that help you turn all the kabobs at once. The skewers are made of metal, wood, or bamboo. Soak wood or bamboo skewers in water for at least 30 minutes before use so they don't burn.

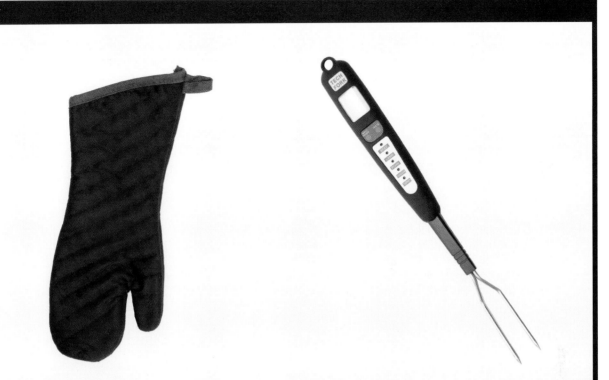

Mitts protect hands from hot utensils. They're better and safer than hot pads, because they cover wrists and lower arms. They're also less likely to slip off or droop near the flames and catch fire.

Thermometers read the temperature of food to prevent over- and under-cooking. The most popular are electronic thermometers built into serving forks. Skewer the meat and read the temperature in the LCD window in the handle.

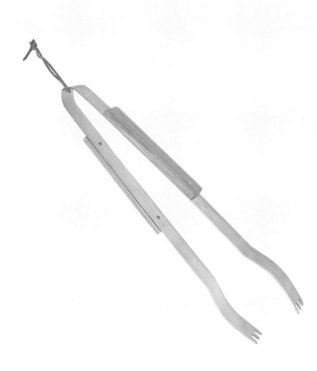

Tongs turn everything from hot dogs to steaks. Look for stainless-steel and teak wood construction for long life.

Other tools might include a grill brush to scrape the grate of burned bits and various spatulas for differently shaped foods.

Built-In Drawer Base

The more ambitious your plans for preparing and serving food in an outdoor kitchen, the more functional your project should be. This is especially true of storage—at least if you want the convenience of having utensils, ingredients, and other items close at hand. Grill bases and other support structures typically have some enclosed space available for storage. It's usually just an open bay with perhaps a pair of metal doors to keep stored items out of sight.

You'd never put up with that kind of limited and inconvenient storage in an indoor kitchen. Setting up shop outdoors calls for some of the same indoor amenities. Drawers are especially useful; they help organize utensils and other small items, and they bring the contents forward so you don't have to go hunting through an undercounter cabinet to find them. A single waist-high drawer is a must for an efficient and well-equipped outdoor kitchen; better still, build in a modular drawer bank with three or four drawers.

A drawer bay offers indoor-kitchen storage capacity and convenience outdoors—and it looks well-organized.

A BUILT-IN DRAWER BASE

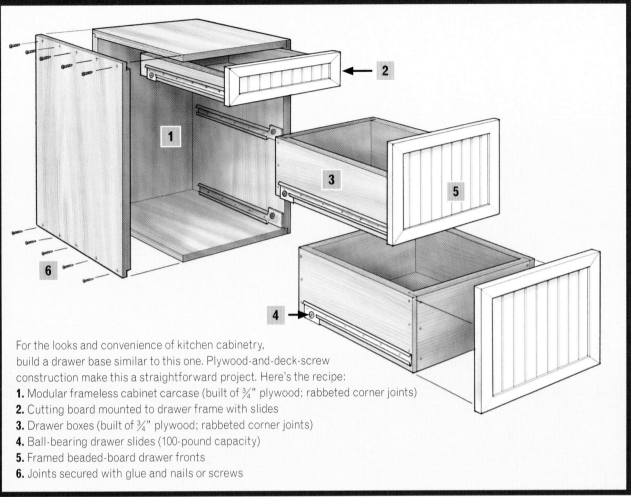

For the looks and convenience of kitchen cabinetry, build a drawer base similar to this one. Plywood-and-deck-screw construction make this a straightforward project. Here's the recipe:

1. Modular frameless cabinet carcase (built of ¾" plywood; rabbeted corner joints)
2. Cutting board mounted to drawer frame with slides
3. Drawer boxes (built of ¾" plywood; rabbeted corner joints)
4. Ball-bearing drawer slides (100-pound capacity)
5. Framed beaded-board drawer fronts
6. Joints secured with glue and nails or screws

DESIGN AND MATERIALS

The conventional materials of indoor cabinetry work well for most outdoor kitchen applications provided there's some protection from rain and direct sun. Fluctuations in humidity will be much greater outdoors, so the materials' dimensional stability is critical. If you've ever had a swollen cabinet or entry door stick when the weather gets wet or muggy, you know the effects of water on wood. Properly finished exterior-grade plywoods offer more stability and longevity than solid-wood components, which will shrink and swell more as the weather changes. If you must have the look of solid wood for cabinet facades and other details, keep the board widths narrow and use traditional frame-and-panel construction for doors, drawer fronts, and other large components.

Because of exposure to the weather, the base of an outdoor kitchen is usually built using masonry materials (brick, block, or stone) or sometimes stainless steel. Some kitchens feature wood framing but are wrapped in these more durable exteriors. Whatever the construction type, allow for modular storage features. This simply means leaving designated bays where storage cabinets can be installed as complete units and/or changed out easily if storage needs or preferences change later.

This example houses three drawers inside a plywood enclosure or carcass. Built from ¾-inch plywood and assembled with glued rabbet joints and deck screws, the carcass offers a sturdy surround for the drawers and allows the use of heavy-duty metal drawer slides. This type of hardware is unaffected by humidity and easily handles loads up to 100 pounds. Full-extension versions allow pulling the drawer completely clear of the base for easier access to the contents. As in this example the top drawer can be fitted with a wood or plastic cutting board—either material is friendlier to knife edges than the stone countertop.

Dressing up the drawers (also of plywood construction) lets you pick details and colors that work with the rest of your outdoor kitchen. Here, panels that look like beaded-board are edged with 1×2 hardwood frames that are mitered at the corners.

5

Planning Your

Here's where the fun really begins—turn your vision of an outdoor kitchen into a building plan.

There are so many options to consider: Where do you place a kitchen to take best advantage of the landscape, the view, the garden, and any other amenities a backyard has to offer? What kind of layout best suits the nature of the cooking and entertaining that will be done there? How—and to what extent—do you equip an outdoor kitchen for storage, cooking, preparation, dining, and cleanup functions?

Finally there's the pleasure of sitting down and mapping it all out, putting ideas on paper in the form of a building plan that will guide the outdoor kitchen's construction.

It's time to get started!

Outdoor Kitchen

The Big Picture

Even if you already think you know exactly where to put an outdoor kitchen, keep an open mind for the moment. Tour the yard, deck, patio, or pool area as if for the first time and ask yourself: Where would I like to cook? To eat? To entertain? Sometimes your initial impulse is best, but sometimes it can be improved. First consider the poetic—the light, view, surroundings, and smells. Then pay attention to more prosaic concerns—proximity to utility hookups, traffic patterns, and topography.

MAKING A BASE MAP

Start planning with a base map—an overhead diagram of the property that includes property lines and major features, such as the house, outbuildings, and trees. The easiest way to go about developing a base map is to make a scaled copy of your plat or other official map. You might find such a map among the papers from the closing of your home. Get a copy from the county tax assessor. In many communities the tax assessor has a website from which to download a map of your lot, including the footprint of the house and any appendages and outbuildings such as garages.

WHAT THE BASE MAP SHOULD SHOW

• The distance of major elements, such as trees, the house, a garden shed, or a detached garage, from the property lines and from each other
• Location of doors and windows in each room
• The overhang of roof eaves beyond the walls of the house (if you are building a new deck or patio as part of the project)
• Downspouts and runoff direction
• Topography—the direction and pitch of slopes or major changes in the ground level

BUBBLE AND MASTER PLANS

A bubble plan shows how to use different areas in a yard. A master plan shows all the elements in the landscape design, both the hardscape and the planting beds. Both plans are handy if building an outdoor kitchen as part of a landscape makeover. If you are simply adding a kitchen to an existing plan, skip these plans and make scale drawings of the project.

To make the bubble plan, tape tracing paper over a base map. Mark different areas of the yard by drawing circles or ovals, then label how each one is used. Tape another piece of tracing paper over the base map to make the master plan. Draw all the landscape details on the plan.

The first step in planning an outdoor kitchen is to make a base map of the yard.

Most outdoor kitchens are either freestanding or attached to the main residence—but there may be other options. This one adds beauty and functionality to a poolhouse. The new kitchen taps into existing plumbing and utilities, and creates a flowing dining/relaxing/entertaining area toward the back of the property. The structure offers a better view and more seclusion than a kitchen attached to the main house.

Marking the Restrictions

Next call your planning and zoning department and utility company and ask what, if any, restrictions apply to your project. Draw these restrictions on the base map. Some planning and zoning restrictions might include:

• **Setbacks.** Setback requirements mandate the number of feet between the building area and the property line. Setbacks are designed to provide adequate space between buildings for light, ventilation, access, and privacy. Most residential areas require 10 or more feet from the side property boundary to the buildable area. Setbacks for the front and rear are usually greater and depend on the size of the lot. The best way to check your setback restrictions is to review your lot's survey plat. If you do not have a copy, request one from the local municipality authority.

• **Easements.** An easement is a legal interest in a parcel of land that is owned by someone other than the landowner. The homeowner does not own the rights to the land use on an easement even though it is on his or her property. For example, utility companies most likely have easements on your lot so that they can run sewer or power lines on your

BUILDING CODES

Before planning an outdoor kitchen, visit area building departments. Meet briefly with local building code officials to see if your project requires a building permit and to make sure it won't violate zoning restrictions. A rough sketch of the project will make the visit even more productive.

An existing deck offers a logical and economical site for an outdoor kitchen because site preparation work is completed. Building a new deck to accommodate an outdoor kitchen also makes sense and often can be the least expensive option for a steeply sloping or uneven site.

If you're planning on making a number of landscaping changes when you build your outdoor kitchen, you may want to hire a landscape designer to come up with a comprehensive plan for your yard at the same time.

property. Permanent structures may not be placed on most easement areas.

• **Utility Lines.** Call the local utility companies—gas, electricity, water, and telephone—to have them mark underground utility lines on your property. It is crucial to know where these lines are even if you are excavating only a few inches. Depths of the lines can vary. Many states offer a one-call service for utility marking; call the North American One Call Referral System at 888/258-0808. Ask to have the route and depth of each utility line marked. Also find and mark all sprinkler lines and outdoor lighting wires if you have those.

HIGH-TECH PLANNING

Landscape design software can simplify a redesign job. These programs are easy to use and flexible and can speed progress from base plan to final design. They are especially useful when making changes because plans can be altered without redrawing.

The programs calculate dimensions of each structure, create side elevations and three-dimensional views, list materials, and create repeating patterns on walkways. Trees and shrubs can also be put in place.

Home improvement and gardening magazines often review the newest software available at computer stores. Or check out local home improvement or building supply centers. Many offer computer design services free of charge if materials are purchased there.

Aesthetic Concerns

Before looking for a spot on which to build a project, consider your lot as a whole. Draw the results of your analysis on the base map as you go.

Build on the north of the lot. In a study in a Berkeley, California neighborhood, residents were shown a plan of their lots and asked to circle the areas in which they spent the most time. In nearly every case, they circled areas with a southern exposure. Like plants we are drawn to the sunlight. Make the most of your yard by building your outdoor kitchen on its northern edge, leaving the sunny southern stretch for outdoor living. Building a project against the southern edge of a property, on the other hand, puts your project at the mercy of your neighbor, who may decide to plant trees, build a fence, or construct an outbuilding that could shade the structure.

Inventory the lot's best features. Walk your lot carefully at various times of day to get a sense of what you like best about it and what you don't want to disturb with the outdoor kitchen project. Tie bright orange ribbon around trees and plants you want to preserve. If there are some exceptional plants or small trees in the route of a new path or patio created by your project, consider marking them with a different color ribbon for transplanting.

Note your lot's worst features. All parts of a lot are often not in equally good condition. Perhaps a concrete slab from an old garage is present, for example. Consider redeeming such places by putting your outdoor kitchen there. This displaces the damage, avoids disrupting your lot's best features, and eliminates the expense of repairing the damage. For example, using an existing slab in good condition for the foundation of a patio can save a great deal of trouble and money.

Account for the wind. Extend your outdoor kitchen's seasonal use by careful planning. Place cabinetry, walls, chimneys, or other structural features where they provide shelter from cool-weather winds. If you live in a hot climate, you might be able to place your kitchen facing cooling summer breezes.

Create outdoor rooms. When siting your outbuilding, envision the shapes it will leave on your lot. People feel most comfortable when there's some sense of containment, and prefer courtyards, for example, to wide-open spaces. Make the most of this preference for intimacy by placing your outdoor kitchen and adjacent dining or gathering areas so they work with your house, garage, and any walls, fences, or other yard features. To make your outdoor rooms even more attractive, reduce noise and increase privacy by placing either your outbuilding or a sturdy fence between your yard and a busy street, for example.

This outdoor kitchen shows careful planning. A fireplace and chimney separate the cooking area from the sitting zone shielding guests from heat, smoke, and moisture. The result is an inviting, shaded sitting area near the pool.

Create outdoor rooms. People feel more comfortable with a sense of enclosure, so balance your desire for a sweeping view with some boundaries. This hilltop kitchen's gathering area uses a see-through steel fence and a half-wall of low plantings to create the feel of a room without obscuring the vista.

Minimize noise. A strategically placed shed can block traffic noise, for instance, creating a relatively quiet oasis in your yard. You'll want to place a dining area away from excessive background noise so you can enjoy relaxed conversation with family and guests.

Assess the view. Note the best vistas on your lot, and think about placing a kitchen to take advantage of them. Also ponder how to use your kitchen or its structures, such as a pergola, wall, or chimney, to block an unattractive aspect of your neighbor's yard or to provide increased privacy.

Work with the topography. Level ground makes it easier to create structural elements, such as a concrete slab or a block wall. A slope or rough terrain still can provide a good spot for a kitchen, but you'll need to factor increased site-preparation costs into the budget. Terracing, for instance, can counteract a slope; a deck supported by individual concrete piers can deal with rough ground. A sloped site raises other issues. If building on the upper levels, you may lose privacy or end up with exposure to excess wind. Build on low ground and you'll have to manage drainage and water runoff. All of these issues can be controlled, but it's best to think them through before construction begins.

Become familiar with the common weather patterns for the microclimate in your yard. Note seasonal temperatures, prevailing winds, the location and angle of the sun at different times of the year, and average rainfall. These conditions can help you determine everything from the best orientation for the kitchen to what type of shelter you'll need. Although built-in features and shelter add to the project cost, they'll also extend the season for outdoor cooking and dining.

Armed with colored pencils and a garden template, embellish a bird's-eye view drawing of an outdoor kitchen with the landscaping components. Then add the footprint of the proposed kitchen, along with any enhancements such as fences, paths, or plants.

Building an Attached Outdoor Kitchen

Attaching an outdoor kitchen to your home's exterior can drastically lower the costs for getting power and water to your kitchen. This is especially true if you can locate the outdoor kitchen on the same wall as the indoor kitchen.

Here limited space on the pool deck would keep the kitchen close to the house anyway, so tethering it directly makes sense. With the pool occupying the convenient middle ground, a detached kitchen would be inconvenient and remote, stuck on the far side of the pool area. Instead the homeowners chose a relatively idle area near the end of the house and created a cross-gable roof to shelter the grill, sink, and appliances.

DESIGN AND MATERIALS

Of course it's possible to build an outdoor kitchen without a roof. The more features added to a project, the more likely the need for protection from weather. An existing roof projection over a patio may offer sufficient cover; otherwise, look for likely spots to connect a new roof assembly to your house. The simplest route is to extend a gable roof further from the house or to attach a new

roof section to the upper area of an exterior wall without disturbing the main roof. A cross-gable addition like the one shown here, however, allows more headroom.

Striking a balance between the house and addition is critical. A cross-gable or shed roof can add architectural interest, but scale it down so the main roof stays dominant. Select a roof slope that repeats an angle from elsewhere on the house.

This kitchen borrows heavily from the existing exterior details to make a pleasing connection. The exposed oversize rafters and other large timbers give it dimension and character, and the split stone base facade and simple gray/white color scheme create a stylistic link with the house.

Even with the wide roof overhangs, windblown rain or snow will make it occasionally into the kitchen area, so stainless-steel fixtures and granite countertops help ensure the project will be durable and easy to clean. Utility lines run through the exterior wall have only a short journey to their connections, which simplifies the design and lowers construction costs.

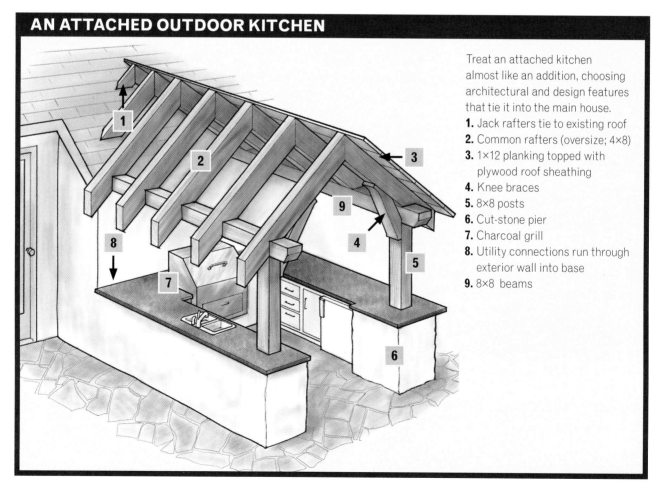

AN ATTACHED OUTDOOR KITCHEN

Treat an attached kitchen almost like an addition, choosing architectural and design features that tie it into the main house.

1. Jack rafters tie to existing roof
2. Common rafters (oversize; 4×8)
3. 1×12 planking topped with plywood roof sheathing
4. Knee braces
5. 8×8 posts
6. Cut-stone pier
7. Charcoal grill
8. Utility connections run through exterior wall into base
9. 8×8 beams

This attached kitchen backs up to a house wall that contains water and electric utilities, making lighting and plumbing connections easy and affordable. A gable roof provides maximum headroom.

The Details

Now that you've considered where to put your outdoor kitchen, it's time to focus on its precise design and the look of related spaces such as dining and gathering areas.

Most outdoor kitchens are neither fully equipped nor used daily, so they usually don't involve the complexity of a home's main indoor kitchen. There are still basic functional categories to borrow from mainstream kitchen design: storage, food preparation, cooking, dining, and cleanup. Not all these functions are required of an outdoor kitchen, especially if you want only a grilling station, but it's best to include as many as possible during the initial planning stages. If you end up wanting a simpler design, the extraneous features can be eliminated.

It is best to come up with three or more possible plans for an outdoor kitchen. The more times you repeat the planning exercise, the more options you'll discover. You may end up picking the first design, the last design—or creating an additional design that combines the best features of all of the plans.

For a better idea of what a project will look like when completed, hire a landscape designer or architect to create a project rendering—a colored drawing that shows the features, including structural elements and landscaping. Halfway between a plan and a painting, its cost can be worthwhile for complex projects such as this one, as it can alert you to changes to make before construction begins.

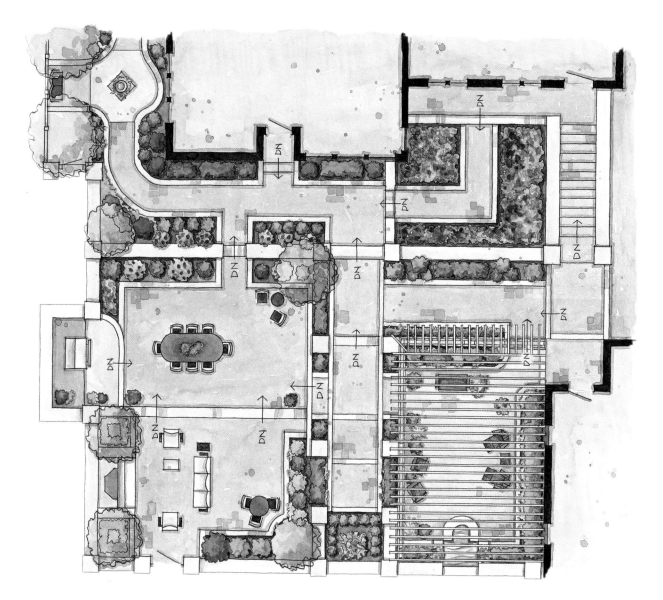

A simple scale drawing will determine what will fit on a site. Use pencil, graph paper, and a few rudimentary drawing implements such as pencil, compass, and a French curve.

Think beyond your first plan. Do at least three drawings with different layouts, then combine the best features or pick a favorite. Brainstorm past the first, most obvious ideas to come up with good alternatives.

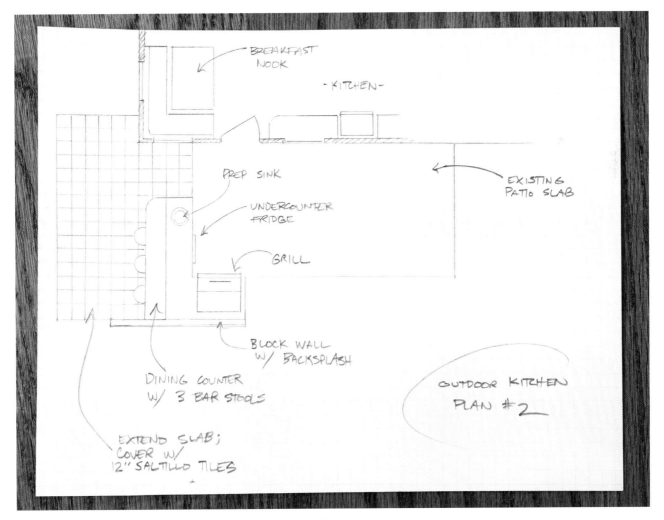

Once settled on a plan, run it by local building officials who must approve the design and issue a permit. They can quickly identify code issues that will be involved with the project.

Building a Glazed Roof

This attached kitchen's defining feature is the wood and glass roof that keeps it dry without casting a shadow over cookouts. Perched on a deck, it also features handsome wood cabinetry supporting the grill and prep areas.

Conservatories and public greenhouses use glass roofs to create a healthy environment for plants and a wonderful transition between indoors and out. You can borrow the principle to achieve the same effect. Done on a modest scale, such a roof is moderately affordable. Better still it helps ensure getting your money's worth out of the investment in a kitchen.

DESIGN AND MATERIALS

The framing for this project is similar to a conventional roof, but with everything exposed you will likely want to splurge on better grades of lumber. This version is a hip roof—more complicated than a gable roof but still buildable by a competent carpenter. The inside portions of the roof slope upward and nest in a corner formed by the exterior walls of the house. (See illustration, page 139.)

A glazed roof introduces safety and code issues, so check with local building officials to see what is required. If using glass, it will have to be tempered and of a specified minimum thickness that depends on the unsupported area. Tempered glass can't be cut so every piece has to be custom-ordered to required specifications after the frame is designed or built. It's usually a good idea to specify tinted glass for overhead applications to keep the space from overheating.

An alternative to tempered glass is polycarbonate panels. This durable plastic is highly impact-resistant but some varieties can yellow over time. They are lightweight and less expensive than glass and are used regularly in residential greenhouses.

A glazed roof offers an abundance of light and a wide-open view combined with shelter from the weather. The conservatory look can be achieved by a variety of methods using readily available materials.

A GLAZED ROOF

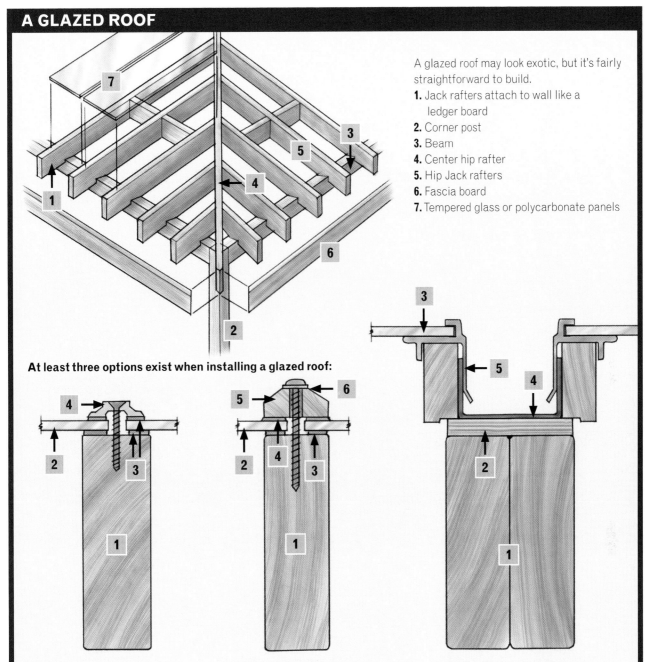

A glazed roof may look exotic, but it's fairly straightforward to build.
1. Jack rafters attach to wall like a ledger board
2. Corner post
3. Beam
4. Center hip rafter
5. Hip Jack rafters
6. Fascia board
7. Tempered glass or polycarbonate panels

At least three options exist when installing a glazed roof:

Option 1. Have a modular system professionally installed. Some manufacturers make specialized components for glass roofs including complete systems with extruded aluminum channels and watertight gaskets that can be installed on top of a wood frame built on site. Local glass shops often sell and install these systems. Alternatively use readily available generic components for the same outcome.
1. Rafter (end view)
2. Tempered glass
3. Watertight gaskets
4. Aluminum channel

Option 2. Build a system using common materials—caulking, weatherstripping, dimension lumber, and wood screws—from a home center. Allow some room for the glass panels to shift or expand without the edges butting against hardware or each other.
1. Rafter (end view)
2. Tempered glass
3. Adhesive weatherstrip
4. Clear silicone caulk
5. Wood channel with oversize holes
6. Flat washer under screw head

Option 3. Use manufactured skylights. These feature integral flashing systems and gaskets and often can be installed as quickly as modular components, although some may require framing modifications such as double rafters.
1. Double 2-by rafters (or use 4-by stock)
2. Plywood sheathing
3. Tempered glass
4. U-channel flashing
5. Extruded aluminum skylight frame overlaps flashing

6

Materials and

A mosaic of materials adds interest to this hilltop outdoor kitchen. The pool and hot tub feature cobblestone rims whose texture and variegated color contrast nicely with the smooth, glazed paver tiles that cover the patio and walkway areas. In keeping with its southwestern location, adobe stucco and weathered wood create the kitchen enclosure; a column of carved stone anchors one end of the pergola over the cooking area. Container plantings and vases of cut flowers contribute to the feel of an oasis.

Landscaping

Brick

Warm, earthy brick has a classic look that blends with many house styles. Its durability makes it ideal for outdoor use and its modular shape is handy for building chimneys and fireplaces, walls and walks, patios and planters. It comes in many colors and sizes, is moderately priced, and readily available. Here are a few things you should know:

Grades. Not all bricks meet the same standards for weathering. Moderate weather (MW) bricks are less expensive and more porous, which can cause them to chip or break if exposed to repeated freeze-thaw cycles. In damp, shady conditions they're also inclined to grow moss, a feature some people find charming. Severe weather (SW) bricks withstand temperature extremes and high moisture conditions and are more resistant to staining.

The walls, patio, paths, pergola piers, fireplace, and chimney of this kitchen are all brick. This homeowner specified used brick, as it instantly "ages" the project to more nearly match the vintage house; white-painted bricks scattered throughout the vertical elements make a nice transition from the sun-dappled white pergola to the brick-red floor.

BRICK PATTERNS AND TYPES

Wire cut bricks have a rough texture that adds shadow detail to otherwise uniform walls.

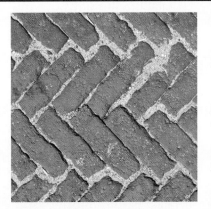

Used pavers have a weathered, tumbled appearance that lends character to this herringbone-set walkway.

The uniform shape and sharp edges of these new paving bricks give a crisp geometric look to this basket-weave pattern patio.

Types. *Common brick* is used primarily for walls and does not hold up to heavy traffic or temperature extremes if used for patios. *House brick* contains large holes that make it lighter to handle but unsuitable for patios. *Paving brick* is made with a dense clay fired at high temperatures making it the hardest, most moisture resistant, and durable brick of all. *Used brick* of all varieties adds a weathered character many find appealing.

Cost, availability, workability. Because it's a manufactured material of regular dimensions, brick is readily available and is easily handled. Its weight means that it is not economical to ship great distances, so regional variations abound. Most masons are intimately familiar with brickwork and many do-it-yourselfers can achieve fine results. Required tools are either inexpensive or can be rented economically.

For more information on working with brick, see pages 150-153.

Carefully matching the type, style, and pattern of brick is important when integrating brick outdoor kitchen features with existing brick construction. Here, aged brick in a running bond pattern unifies the new kitchen island with the home and patio.

Brick Veneer

Brick is a classic landscape material and a natural choice for use in outdoor kitchen structures. It's relatively inexpensive, very durable, and conveys a look of quality that few other materials rival. There can be substantial cost, however, in installation. Laying brick is a labor-intensive job that can't be hurried without sacrificing quality; a good mason will be skilled and efficient, but the process still takes time. Considering the value it adds to a home, though, brickwork is a good investment.

Brick is traditionally both a structural and finish material rather than a decorative veneer added to a block or woodframe structure. It can be used for projects such as planters, low landscape walls, and even for outdoor kitchen bases—if the scale is modest. Each horizontal layer of brick is called a course, and the wall thickness is the wythe. Single-wythe brick structures have limited stability and must be kept low, typically up to 2 feet high depending on the design. Building double-wythe walls, with brick mortared back-to-back in a thick wall, adds strength and allows for taller walls.

The arrangement of bricks is called the pattern, and there are many variations. Most, like the common "running bond" pattern, feature staggered or offset joints from one course to another, so that each brick straddles the joint between the bricks directly above and below. This pattern distributes weight loads more effectively and creates a stronger wall.

Brick works well with just about any other structural or finish material. Here it's paired with a granite countertop and stainless-steel grill. Whitewashing the brick tones down the contrast.

Brick makes sense in an outdoor kitchen, especially if the property already features a brick house, walls, patio, or other brick features. There are several approaches to building with brick, each offering advantages of cost, durability, or ease of construction.

Brick is a versatile material that offers the builder many construction options. Here are four of the most popular. Each has its advantages and drawbacks, so study all four before you make your choice.

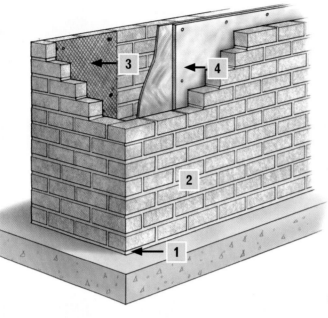

Option 2: Full-Brick Veneer on Woodframe Base

Brick homes typically feature this type of construction. The wall structure consists of wood framing and plywood sheathing covered with housewrap, builder's felt, or a similar moisture barrier. The brick is installed as a decorative outside layer called a veneer. The brick is not attached directly to the wall, however; a gap of at least 1 inch is used to allow ventilation and to keep water that might make its way past the brick away from the inner wall. This also allows the two wall layers to move somewhat independently of each other, a useful precaution given the tendency of wood to shift with changes in humidity. Corrugated metal clips are screwed or nailed to the plywood sheathing, then bent and embedded in the mortar layers between brick courses.

A bit more complex but more sturdy, full-brick veneer on a wood frame allows building higher, stronger walls. Here are the elements involved:

1. Concrete slab (minimum 4" thick)
2. Wire reinforcing mesh
3. Joint mortared to concrete slab
4. 1" air gap
5. Pressure-treated mudsill; attached to concrete slab with anchor bolts
6. 2-by stud frame
7. Corrugated metal ties secure back siding to wall sheathing; bed in mortar joints every other course; 16" on center
8. Weep holes (gaps) allow water to drain; ventilation
9. ¾" exterior plywood sheathing
10. 30-pound builder's felt

Option 1: Reinforced Brick

This technique uses single-wythe construction and so will limit the height of the structure you can build. Without reinforcement, a reasonable height limit is about 2 feet, less if the structure is a planter or low retaining wall with a soil load bearing against the sides. To reinforce the wall use masonry anchors to attach metal lath to the inside of the wall, then trowel a thick coat of mortar onto the lath. Or apply a scratch coat of mortar to the inside wall face, then embed a ½-inch-thick cement board panel in the mortar and attach with masonry anchors. These measures add reinforcement to the wall, but this type of construction still should be considered only for light-duty applications.

For a low, light-duty wall, single-wythe brick construction may be all that's needed. Building is quite straightforward:

1. Mortar joint to concrete slab
2. Standard brick in running bond pattern (limit structure to less than 3' tall)
3. Option A: Metal lath is attached to inside face; trowel mortar into lath
4. Option B: Mortar scratch coat is applied; bed ½" cement board in mortar and attach with anchor/screws

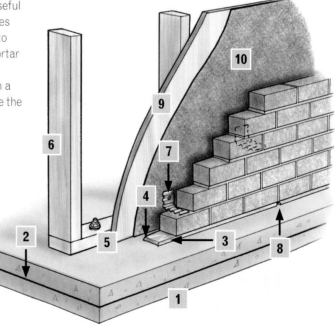

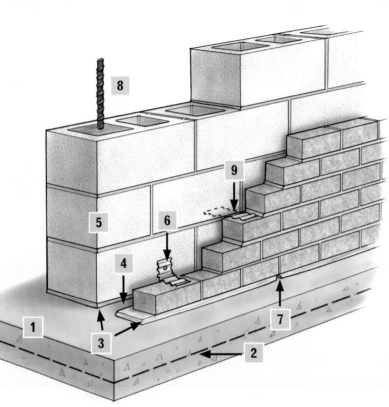

Option 3: Full-Brick Veneer on Concrete Block

This construction method is similar to Option 2, but uses concrete block as the structural wall material. Properly reinforced, this construction is stronger so it's often used for commercial or public buildings. An air gap is included here also, in part to keep excess lime residue from the concrete blocks from leaching into the brick. Similar metal ties are used to connect the two layers; they can be fastened to the block with masonry anchors or where the block and brick courses align, embedded in the mortar joints of both, as shown.

The strongest brick veneer walls are reinforced with concrete block and have these components:

1. Concrete slab (minimum 4" thick)
2. Wire reinforcing mesh
3. Mortar joints
4. 1" to 2" air gap
5. Concrete block structural wall
6. Metal ties attached with screws and anchors
7. Weep holes for drainage and ventilation
8. ½" rebar
9. Where block/brick courses align, corrugated metal ties are embedded in mortar joints

Option 4: Thin-Brick Veneer on Concrete Block

Thin-brick veneer has been around for decades, providing an economical alternative to traditional brick veneer. Typically about ½-inch thick, these veneers are relatively expensive, but they install much like ceramic tile and so represent a significant savings in labor costs over full brick. Special L-shape pieces install at corners and create the appearance of full bricks. Depending on the manufacturer's recommendations, a coat of thinset mortar or mastic adhesive is troweled onto the block surface to embed the bricks. This is an especially user-friendly product for do-it-yourself project builders, and most vendors offer several styles and colors.

For an easy-to-build project with a brick look, thin-brick veneer is the way to go. Here's how to put it together:

1. Concrete slab (minimum 4" thick)
2. ½" gap left above slab
3. Wrap-around corner pieces
4. Block joints troweled flat
5. ½" rebar as required
6. Mastic adhesive applied with notched trowel
7. Thin-brick veneer

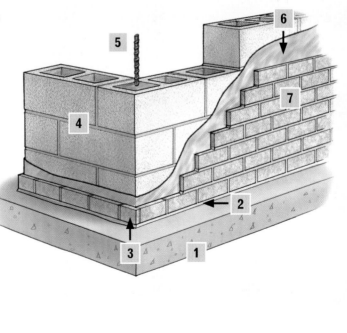

Concrete

Concrete is an inexpensive, versatile material that can be used by itself or in combination with other surfacing materials such as decorative edges made of brick, rock, or tile. It can be finished in many colors and textures, or stamped while still wet to resemble other materials, such as brick or stone. Using forms or molds, concrete also can be cast into walls, benches, and planters that will last a lifetime with little maintenance. Concrete also is cast into decorative blocks and pavers.

Types. *Broom finished* surfaces are swept with a stiff-bristle broom when wet. The resulting surface is roughened and provides excellent traction. *Exposed aggregate* surfaces are sprinkled with small pebbles while still wet, creating a rustic, pebbly texture that is both attractive and offers good traction when wet. Pavers mimic brick, stone,

cobbles, and adobe and are very durable. *Pigments and stains* can be added to the concrete either as it is mixed, while it is wet, or after it cures to create a variety of color effects. *Smooth* concrete can be slippery when wet and is not recommended for outdoor surfaces. *Stamped* concrete is created by making impressions with plastic molds in the concrete while it is still wet, leaving impressions that resemble brick, tile, or stone.

Cost, availability, workability. Whether poured or in block or paver form, concrete is generally less expensive than stone and brick and is available everywhere. Large areas are best poured by professionals; small projects can be poured by do-it-yourselfers with rented equipment. Blocks and pavers are very DIY-friendly.

CONCRETE TYPES AND FINISHES

Rough-faced concrete retaining wall block is inexpensive and easy to install.

These pavers resemble tumbled stone. Like most modular concrete products, they're available in a variety of colors.

Exposed-aggregate concrete offers the color, texture, and durability of a pebble surface.

Even up close, stamped, colored concrete is a convincing imitation of cleft-face stone.

Stained, textured concrete can mimic brick, tile, or stone—at a fraction of the price.

Laying a Brick or Paver Patio

Even though a concrete slab often makes a better and more stable base for an outdoor kitchen (especially one with underground utility connections), brick or paver patios are favorites for other outdoor floor areas. They're less disruptive to install, offer more character than a gray slab, and are within reach of most handy do-it-yourselfers.

Paver patios have an additional virtue: structural flexibility. Individually set bricks or blocks can "float" in place as the ground beneath rises or sinks with seasonal fluctuations in temperature and moisture. Frost-heaving of the soil can crack even reinforced concrete slabs, but often won't disturb a properly installed paver surface. The key is using crushed rock and sand beneath the pavers so they won't sink into muddy soil.

Speaking of muddy, the nomenclature of bricks and pavers has loosened over the years. Traditionally a paver was a particular kind of brick, made of clay but formulated and kiln-fired at higher temperatures to be much denser than a common brick. Tough enough to withstand the traffic of horse-drawn and motor vehicles, they were used to surface urban streets before asphalt and concrete became common. Now the term "pavers" can refer to any uniformly sized masonry blocks made of clay, cut stone, or colored concrete that are used for surfacing driveways, patios, and roads.

This dry-laid brick paver patio's herringbone pattern complements the formal furnishings, topiary, and linear arrangement of a courtyard-like back garden.

A PAVER PATIO

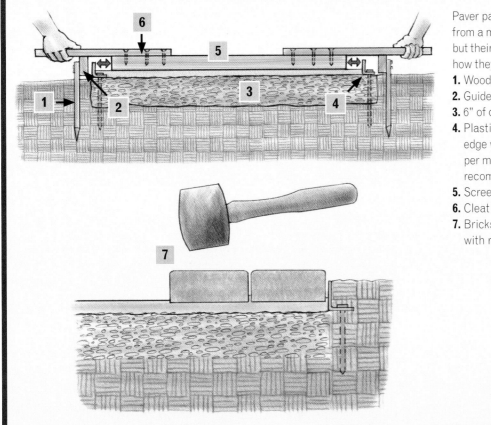

Paver patios get their good looks from a mix of paver and pattern, but their durability comes from how they are laid.

1. Wood stakes
2. Guide form
3. 6" of compacted crushed rock
4. Plastic or metal brick edge with spikes (install per manufacturer's recommendation)
5. Screed board
6. Cleat handles
7. Bricks seated into sand with rubber mallet

A mortared, basket-weave brick patio set off by a jack-on-jack border provides a stable, easy-to-clean surface for this outdoor dining area.

To prep the area, first scrape off the softest layer of topsoil. This may be just a few inches or as much as a foot thick. Then set some stakes and/or guide boards to help you gauge the finished height of the patio and determine how much fill material you'll need to add.

Replace most of the soil with crushed rock. Regional factors will determine what types and sizes are available. Rock that averages smaller than 1 inch in size is easier to place, but don't use pea gravel or anything else that small. The ideal material will allow water drainage but still pack firmly, and the sharp angular faces of mechanically crushed rock give it those properties. Some quarries and vendors sell the stone unwashed, meaning it still has the small chips and fine dust that the crushing process yields. This material packs so well it's often used as a base under roads and highways, though it doesn't drain quite as quickly as washed stone.

The biggest long-term threat to paver installation is uneven or excessive settling, which rock subbase is there to prevent. The rock should be placed in layers (called lifts) about 2 or 3 inches thick, then compacted with a vibrating plate compactor before more rock is added. If you or your contractor skip this step, gravity and time will do it for you with far less predictable results. Add and compact the rock until the top layer is shy of the upper edge of the guide boards by about 1 inch plus the thickness of your pavers. This is also the time to install plastic or metal edging.

A layer of sand provides the final base for the pavers, but as you add it some will disappear into the crushed rock. Run the vibrating compactor over the area again to force it to settle, and add more until about an inch accumulates on the top. This dimension isn't critical, but don't add too much sand; it's there merely to provide some fine adjustment for the individual pavers. Too much sand can be displaced just like soil, causing the pavers to settle unevenly.

Tumbled concrete pavers resemble cobblestone and come in a variety of shapes and colors. Here, square and oblong shapes are combined to create textural interest underfoot.

PAVER PATTERNS

One of the advantages of using pavers is that you can choose from an almost endless variety of paving patterns. Here are a few of the most popular:

Basket weave

Half basket weave

Jack-on-jack

Running bond

Herringbone

Diagonal herringbone

The trick to a flat sand bed is a simple one: Use a straight board called a screed to displace excess sand from the high spots and fill any low spots. (See illustration, page 151.) The screed board should be slightly narrower (top to bottom) than the paver thickness and should have offset handles that rest on the guide boards; the lower edge will level the sand. As the pavers are placed and tamped with a rubber mallet, they'll seat firmly into the sand. After all are placed, more sand gets swept into the joints, followed by several light sprays of water. Some landscaping sand is treated with a water-soluble glue that will activate at this stage, locking the pavers in a stronger matrix.

This technique yields a sturdy but flexible patio surface, and it can be used not only with bricks and masonry pavers but with flagstone and other natural stone materials. If the material thickness is irregular, a thicker sand bed may be required to compensate for the differences in individual stones.

Borders such as this one, which surrounds a concrete paver patio set into a lawn, give the surface a frame or definite edge.

 # Stone

For unmatched natural beauty few materials are as compelling as stone. It comes in many textures and colors and works well with almost any architectural style. Stone varies in hardness, depending upon where it is quarried and the geological forces that formed it. Some sandstone, for instance, is nearly as hard as marble; other types of the same stone can be dented with a fingernail. Stone also varies dramatically in porosity. Stones with a low rate of water absorption are less likely to deteriorate outdoors.

This fireplace surround, hearth, and chimney look like they're made of dry-stacked limestone, but the stone is actually a veneer over a concrete-block masonry structure.

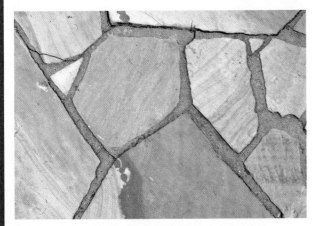

Sandstone flagstone's random shapes and abstract patterns create an attractive patio.

A stone-block stairway edged with boulders offers a rustic-looking way to change elevations on a sloping site.

Limestone block makes an attractive natural retaining wall for flower beds. Uniformly shaped stone blocks can be quickly and easily stacked to form mortarless walls

Varied stone shapes and dimensions create patterned walls that are works of art in themselves, but require great skill and considerable time to construct.

TYPES

Flagstones are flat, natural stones used for walks and patios. Varieties include granite, sandstone, limestone, slate, bluestone, and quartzite. Split-face flagstone, sometimes called cleft-face, creates a rustic look. It has a rough, uneven surface that offers good traction when wet, an important consideration around pools and spas. *Stone tiles* are stones that are cut and shaped by machine into uniform tiles. Marble, slate, sandstone, limestone, and granite are readily available in tile form. Offering a more refined look than irregular flagstones, stone tiles are also smoother and more level, permitting easier rolling of carts and leveling of patio furniture. *River rocks and pebbles* have been worn smooth by water or glaciers. Generally measuring from 1 to 8 inches across, these rocks are extremely durable but are best reserved for decorative accents along the edges of patios or walkways or on vertical surfaces. *Stone blocks* are quarried from solid ledge and are available in a variety of stone types, granite and limestone among the most popular, depending on geographic location. They're great for walls and other structural elements. *Polished slabs* of marble, granite, slate, limestone, and other types of stone are used as premium countertop materials and are available in a wide range of thicknesses and colors.

Cost, availability, workability. The price of stone can vary widely by type and finish; in general, the less processing required, the cheaper the material, so cleft-face flagstone and river rock are among the least expensive; polished countertops are at the high end of the range. Availability is good just about everywhere; types of stone will vary by region. Workability also varies. While just about anyone in good physical condition can lay flagstone, milling custom countertops takes an experienced pro and special equipment, as does working with large blocks. For more information on working with stone, see pages 158-159.

The timeless look of natural stone is matched by its nearly infinite lifespan.

Stone Veneer

Like brick, stone veneer excels at surviving outdoor conditions and creating an upscale look. Properly built stone structures can last centuries, presumably more life than you'll need from your outdoor kitchen. Just as brick is now commonly used as a facade rather than a structural material, rock and stone typically act as decorative and protective veneer on structures built of wood or concrete masonry.

Stone's longevity is due in part to its low porosity, at least for some varieties. Materials that readily absorb water tend to degrade faster than materials that don't. Soft surfaces can erode, but the greater damage usually comes from the expansion of the trapped moisture as it freezes, creating enough force to break solid stones.

On home exteriors stone often is used as an accent, especially on the foundation. Weight and cost are two reasons why use is limited, but there are also aesthetic factors. Large stone structures can look oppressive, more like a fortress than a home. Keeping the stonework below eye level (ideally, between waist and shoulder height) helps prevent this overbuilt look, and the same guideline applies to outdoor kitchen structures.

DESIGN AND MATERIALS

If supporting a heavy countertop or a large built-in grill were the only function of an outdoor kitchen base, you simply could mortar stones into a solid mass. Concealed utility connections and storage areas are usually part of the design, however, so it makes sense to use other more uniform materials to build a structural shell, then apply stone as a decorative veneer.

The substantial weight of stone veneer often dictates using concrete block or concrete walls poured in place rather than woodframe walls for the support structure. For thicker varieties of common stone, a small extension called a brick ledge is often formed into the base of the concrete wall or footing so that the bottom course of stone can rest directly on it. Corrugated metal ties also should be attached to the wall surface and embedded into the mortar joints between stones (see illustration, below). If you aren't sure whether your project requires such support, weigh the stone to see if it exceeds 15 pounds per square foot; if so, use these reinforcements. You also will pay higher freight costs for materials unless they are quarried locally.

A STONE VENEER WALL

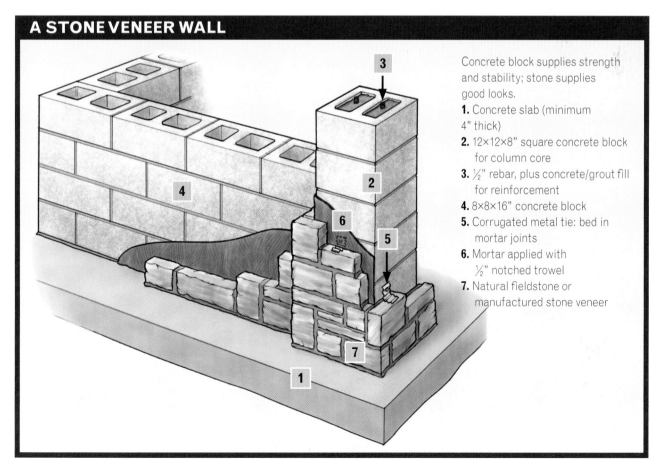

Concrete block supplies strength and stability; stone supplies good looks.

1. Concrete slab (minimum 4" thick)

2. 12×12×8" square concrete block for column core

3. ½" rebar, plus concrete/grout fill for reinforcement

4. 8×8×16" concrete block

5. Corrugated metal tie: bed in mortar joints

6. Mortar applied with ½" notched trowel

7. Natural fieldstone or manufactured stone veneer

The rough-hewn or irregular shape of most natural stones can make some varieties too bulky or rough for smaller projects, but there are alternatives that might be better suited to the scale of an outdoor kitchen. The first is natural thin veneer (NTV), which is simply natural stone that has been sawn or split to create a thinner profile and a flat back. With thicknesses ranging from 1 to 2 inches, NTV can cover a surface with a substantial weight reduction. The flat back also requires less bedding mortar and speeds installation.

Some stones are cut or split even thinner, almost like tiles, and can be installed the same way—without the brick ledge support, metal ties, or thick layer of bedding mortar. They are adhered in thinset mortar and typically don't require additional mortar fill for the joints. The weight reduction with this method opens the option of using a woodframe structure for the support base and attaching cement backerboard as a substrate for the stone tiles.

That construction option also exists for the newest class of materials—manufactured stone veneer made

STONE PATTERNS: DESIGN BEFORE STARTING

Whether it's wildly random shapes and sizes or rough-cut pieces intended for a pattern layout, stone materials should know their place before anyone trowels on the first dab of mortar. Picking stones off the pallet and placing them randomly is likely to result in a poor fit or unattractive/unbalanced patterns. Use rope or string to outline patches of ground that match the size and proportions of the walls and other surfaces to be covered. Experiment with the placement of stone sizes, shapes, and colors at a leisurely pace. Then transfer the stones individually to the intended surfaces. Making these design decisions while placing wet mortar and setting the stones makes the task harder and more prone to error.

The horizontal layers of this stone veneer fireplace seem to grow out of the ground. An armature of concrete blocks makes regular shapes easier to achieve.

Mortared stone veneer offers a more formal look, with a neat geometry and smoother surface than rustic, dry-laid work. It's particularly appropriate in a semi-enclosed space such as this one.

SOURCING YOUR STONE

Stone once was quarried locally. Now natural stone can be transported nationwide or even globally. To avoid excessive freight charges, visit local or regional stone suppliers to find varieties quarried nearby.

Manufactured stone veneer weighs much less than natural stone. These products often are shipped greater distances, so shoppers are not limited to local quarries. Names in this industry include:

- Artistic Stone
- Boulder Creek Stone Products
- Buechel Stone Corp.
- Centurion Stone
- Coronado Stone Products
- Cultured Stone
- El Dorado Stone
- Hammer Stone
- United Stone Veneer

from lightweight concrete. These products are remarkably diverse in style and color and mimic natural stone so convincingly that most people can't tell the difference. Most manufacturers use natural stones to create the molds for their synthetic versions, so the detailing and texture are virtually unchanged. Weighing about one-fourth to one-third of natural stone veneer, these manufactured varieties can be installed without support ledges or metal ties, and special L-shape backs on the corner stones make for easy transitions between surfaces. If installed on woodframe structures, two layers of moisture barrier (roofing felt) are attached first, then a metal lath to provide a good bond for the mortar bed. When that's cured, the stone veneer is applied.

Traditional sparkling-white stucco lightens the interior of this outdoor kitchen's gathering space. Adobe is easily molded to both linear and rounded shapes.

 # Stucco

Stucco makes an excellent exterior surface. A traditional stucco finish is nothing more than two or three thin coats of a mortar that is 1 part masonry cement to 3 parts sand, with a small amount of lime and water added. Stucco requires a solid backing and can accept an infinite variety of final textures that give each stucco finish an old-world, handcrafted appeal that's hard to match.

Types. *Bright white* stucco is made by mixing together white Portland cement, lime, and white silica sand for the finish coat. *Traditional* stucco, if unfinished, dries to a medium gray color. *Pigmented* stucco can be created by adding an oxide pigment to the finish coat. This stucco has a permanent color that permeates the entire finish coat so it won't wear or flake. Pigment must be mixed carefully to ensure uniform color across batches. *Stained* stucco is colored with a liquid stain applied after the finish coat of stucco has cured. *Synthetic* stucco is made from polymers, is easier to apply than traditional stucco, and comes in a variety of colors.

Cost, availability, workability. The materials that make up traditional stucco are universally available and inexpensive. Applying stucco takes practice, but the material is forgiving and the tools are inexpensive. Traditional stucco requires days of misting while drying to prevent cracking, and labor costs for applying three coats and monitoring drying can add up. New polymer stucco materials ease and speed installation but cost more.

STUCCO TYPES AND FINISHES

Traditional colored stucco often features mellow, earthy tones that create an old-world feel, especially when combined with hand-tooled textures.

Dramatic textures such as this one add interest to flat walls, animating them with a play of light and shadow that changes throughout the day.

Stucco also can be smoothed to a near-velvety finish. When stained after the finish coat has dried, tiny cracks in the material give the finish a veined quality similar to marble.

Synthetic stucco made of modern polymers can be as vivid as brightly painted surfaces.

Stucco Finishes

There's a reason so many homes features stucco exteriors. This versatile exterior plaster—made from portland cement, sand, and/or lime mixed with water—is affordable, durable enough to last decades with very little maintenance, and capable of a variety of textures and colors. Color can be integral (mixed into the wet batch) or applied to the surface, and the material's stability allows paint to last.

Stucco has a pedigree nearly as old as that of brick and stone. Early versions were troweled on in multiple layers, covering narrow strips of wood lath that were spaced closely together and nailed to framing timbers. The wet base coat mix oozes into gaps between the lath strips and then hardens, locking the coating securely to the wall. Subsequent coats would add thickness and a flat, smooth surface that could be whitewashed or painted. On today's homes, however, the substrate is a metal wire lath backed by a moisture barrier, such as black roofing felt, and the stucco is often sprayed on rather than troweled. Texture, if any, can be sprayed or hand-applied.

DESIGN AND MATERIALS

If your home has a stucco exterior, there's an obvious advantage in using a matching material for your outdoor kitchen. Stucco's low-profile look, and the ability to match details such as paint color and wood or masonry trim,

Stucco is a low-cost, high-durability finish that mixes well with a variety of architectural styles and outdoor finish materials.

A STUCCO WALL

Here's a cutaway look at stucco as it's applied to two different types of structural walls:

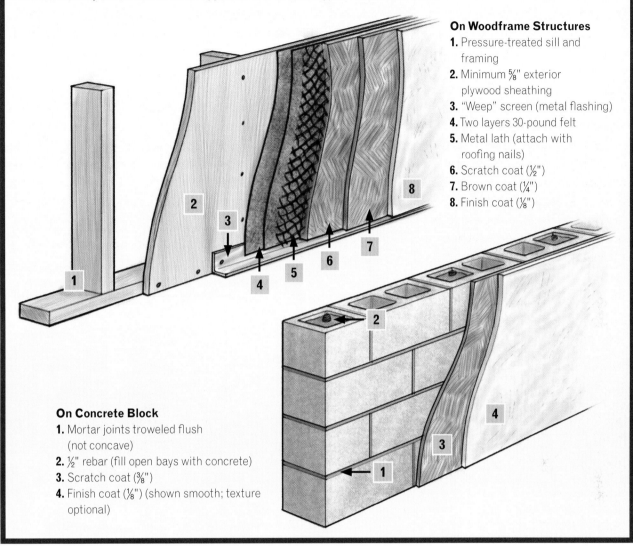

On Woodframe Structures
1. Pressure-treated sill and framing
2. Minimum ⅝" exterior plywood sheathing
3. "Weep" screen (metal flashing)
4. Two layers 30-pound felt
5. Metal lath (attach with roofing nails)
6. Scratch coat (½")
7. Brown coat (¼")
8. Finish coat (⅛")

On Concrete Block
1. Mortar joints troweled flush (not concave)
2. ½" rebar (fill open bays with concrete)
3. Scratch coat (⅜")
4. Finish coat (⅛") (shown smooth; texture optional)

make it easy to integrate a design with other materials that might be featured on your home's exterior.

Stucco is as much a building system as a material. Its layered construction calls for specific steps so that each coat bonds securely to the one beneath. For woodframe structures where the metal lath and paper backing are attached to plywood sheathing, the process requires a thick base called a scratch coat, so named because it is scarified or scratched with a wire comb to create small horizontal ridges. These ridges help the second layer, called the brown coat, to bond to the first and retain moisture. (Like any masonry mix where water causes cement crystals to form, stucco cures stronger and cracks less when it doesn't dry out too quickly at the surface.)

Depending on the stucco mix and site conditions such as temperature and relative humidity, the scratch and brown coats should cure from 2 to 7 days before

proceeding. Covering the surface temporarily with plastic sheeting helps retain moisture. The third, or finish, coat is about 1/8-inch thick.

For masonry surfaces such as concrete block or poured-in-place concrete, a two-coat application (scratch and finish) is all that's required. The substrate wall should be wetted before applying the stucco so it doesn't wick too much moisture from the mix.

As a material and a process, stucco isn't complicated, but it should be installed by professional masons. An experienced hand is needed because the mix proportions for each coat differ slightly, the trowel techniques require practice, and the need for proper curing between coats is essential.

Tile

Tile has limitless potential for pattern and color. Tile rated "impervious" for outdoor use is durable and requires little maintenance but needs a concrete base and considerable labor to install. Tile either can be glazed or unglazed. Unglazed tiles are best for flooring because glazed versions can be slippery—wet or dry.

Types. *Ceramic* floor tile has a ceramic glaze bonded to a clay body. Hardness ratings of 1-4 indicate wall use only; 5 to 6 ratings are appropriate for low-traffic floors; and ratings higher than 6 are good choices for high-traffic floors. *Porcelain* floor tiles are fired at very high temperatures to make them extremely hard and stain resistant. Available glazed or unglazed, some have slip-resistant textures that are ideal for outdoor floors. *Quarry tile* is a tough, durable mixture of clay and shale that's fired at high temperatures. It is unglazed and available in a range of earth tones. *Terra-cotta* tiles have a rustic, handmade look, often featuring uneven edges and surface imperfections that lend character. Generally less durable than quarry tile, they may be appropriate for covered areas and should be sealed if exposed to moisture.

Cost, availability, workability. Tile cost varies widely with the pattern, glaze, and tile origin (their weight makes imports expensive); ceramic tiles are generally least expensive. Installation costs depend on the complexity of the job. DIY installation is possible but requires exacting craftsmanship and some rented tools.

Tile also can play a more subdued role. While the water line and steps of this pool are accented in bright blue to cue bathers to their presence, a mellow, earth-toned tile edges the patio and covers the kitchen's floor.

Brilliant, super-saturated colors are a tile trademark—as are contrasting grout colors, which emphasize the geometric nature of the design.

TILE TYPES AND PATTERNS

Mixing tile types, colors, and finishes is an opportunity to animate outdoor kitchen patio surfaces. Here glazed blue tile contrasts nicely with a field of unglazed tiles in a terra-cotta color.

Glazed brick, a relative of tile, can help add pattern and color to walls and patio surfaces. Indigo-colored, end-glazed brick along with a corner block of limestone punctuates this brick wall.

Want to define an area or give shape to a patio? Add a tile border such as this classic checkerboard.

Tile Countertops

Countertop trends in many of today's designer kitchens call for large slabs of exotic granite or concrete cast in place with inlaid metals and semiprecious stones. These high-end materials also work in most outdoor settings, but you may find more variety and better value with an old standby: ceramic tile.

No other suitable countertop material offers as many design, color, and texture options as ceramic tile, but this proven performer has lost ground to newer and more fashionable goods. The maintenance of grout lines is the drawback mentioned most often. Today's grouts and sealers hold up much better than early-generation products, so don't let that issue steer you away from this otherwise versatile and affordable material.

DESIGN AND MATERIALS

If any characteristic dictates designs using ceramic tiles, it's the rigid nature of the material. Like other masonry products, tile performs well under compressive stresses (weight or pushing forces) if it's adequately and uniformly supported. If it's not properly installed and supported, however, it will crack rather than flex, so the substrate must be rigid and stable.

Good substrates for countertops must be thick enough to resist deflection from normal use. Plywood or similar

Rich colors, a glossy, easy-to-clean surface, and reasonable cost make tile a good choice for outdoor kitchens. Often overlooked these days in favor of trendier polished stone or granite, it's worth consideration.

A TILE COUNTERTOP SUBSTRATE

What's under the tile is as important as the choice of surface. Here's the structural beef behind a good-looking bar countertop:

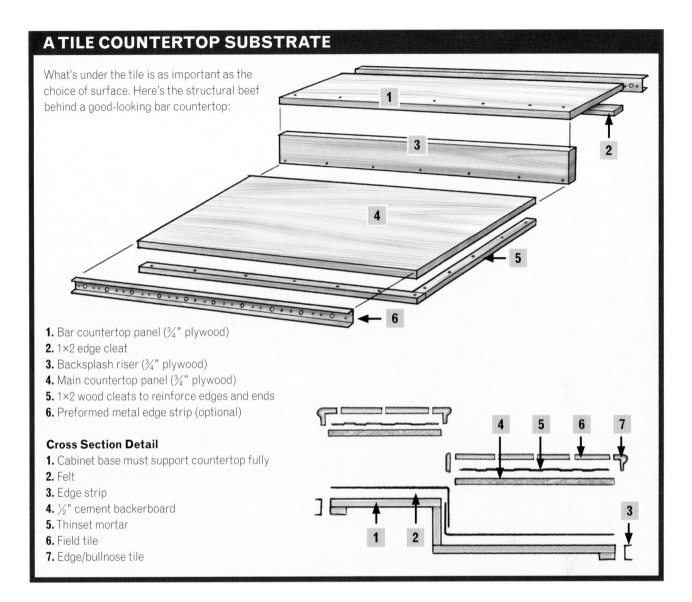

1. Bar countertop panel (¾" plywood)
2. 1×2 edge cleat
3. Backsplash riser (¾" plywood)
4. Main countertop panel (¾" plywood)
5. 1×2 wood cleats to reinforce edges and ends
6. Preformed metal edge strip (optional)

Cross Section Detail
1. Cabinet base must support countertop fully
2. Felt
3. Edge strip
4. ½" cement backerboard
5. Thinset mortar
6. Field tile
7. Edge/bullnose tile

engineered panels (particleboard or medium-density fiberboard [MDF]) are commonly used. These materials should be at least ¾-inch thick and reinforced with wood cleats or other bracing, especially around the perimeter. Make sure the support base or cabinet underneath also has plenty of bracing and cleats to attach the countertops securely.

After the plywood countertop base is installed, other materials directly underneath the tile increase the substrate stability. Sealing both faces and all edges with a polyurethane or waterborne varnish helps keep the plywood stable, although it's an extra step often omitted. A layer of felt underlayment (roofing paper) serves as a moisture barrier, and cement backerboard screwed to the plywood provides an ideal surface for adhering tile. Thinset mortar is troweled onto the backerboard as a bedding material for the tile. Joint spacers and a layout help ensure that the tile stays aligned and in place. Allow the tile to set for 24 hours before grouting.

SIZE MATTERS

Small mosaic-style tiles tend to create more visual interest because of pattern options and the increased contrast with grout lines, but that's not necessarily a good thing for countertops. Large tiles offer bigger sections of flat surface to work on and fewer grout lines to fill and periodically clean. (If tile sizes are too large for a countertop, however, they can look odd and out of scale. Consider including just a few 12×12 or 16×16 tiles for designated work zones and use smaller tiles around them.) Floors benefit from smaller tiles, which crack less under foot traffic and provide more of a slip-resistant surface because of the closely spaced grid of grout lines.

Sealed oak cabinetry and a stained pine overhead structure set off this Arts and Crafts-influenced outdoor kitchen.

Wood

Wood is versatile, attractive, natural, and easy to work with. Several types of wood are used for the decking, railing, cabinetry, planters, pergolas, and built-in furniture found in many outdoor kitchens.

Types. *Cedar* and *cypress* are lightweight, resist rot and decay, and are used for cabinetry and decking. *Ipe* and other tropical hardwoods are strong, dense, highly resistant to weather and insects, and are increasingly popular for decking, cabinetry, and islands. *Pine*, a soft, lightweight wood, should be coated with a clear sealer, stain, or paint prior to installation. *Pressure-treated* wood is used widely for decking, railing, and fencing, and can be stained or painted. *Salvaged* wood such as barn siding and beams adds a rustic, aged look that requires little maintenance.

Cost, availability, workability. Pine and pressure-treated wood is cheapest. Redwood, cedar, and cypress are more expensive. Ipe, a Brazilian walnut, is the most costly. Most species are widely available except for cypress, which is easy to get in the South, and Ipe, which is imported and not available in all markets. Wood is lighter than masonry materials and can be worked with common tools, making it a favorite DIY material. Ipe is more difficult to work than most woods. Its hardness and denseness dulls tools more quickly and can require drilling and countersinking pilot holes for fasteners, which can add considerably to labor costs on large deck projects. Depending upon the source and application, salvaged lumber can require additional labor to detect and remove old fasteners and to clean and resaw into desired dimensions.

WOOD TYPES

Popular wood types include, from top to bottom, left to right: Ipe, decar, redwood, pressure-treated, and pine.

Pressure-treated lumber is long-lasting and accepts stain well, as shown by these steps to an elevated deck.

Painted pine is inexpensive and offers a crisp, clean backdrop for plants such as this climbing honeysuckle.

Salvaged lumber, such as the weathered oak beams repurposed to construct this pergola, adds instant character and does not require painting, staining, or sealing.

Deck with Integrated Grill Island

Outdoor kitchens must accommodate extreme weather conditions with minimum maintenance. Those demands give masonry products such as tile, brick, and stone an edge among building materials—for the kitchen structure or for surrounding features such as patios, retaining walls, and landscaping. Some people still prefer the look and feel of a wood deck for their backyard getaway, and there's every reason an outdoor kitchen design can feature both.

Decks offer greater design flexibility within a budget, both for the size and shape of the space and for built-ins and detailing possibilities. For example, built-in benches with storage underneath are relatively easy and inexpensive to fashion in wood, but masonry alternatives would be costlier and less practical.

On some problem sites with steep or uneven terrain, a raised deck often can provide more usable square footage than a concrete or paver patio design—usually for less money. If your home exterior or landscape already features stone or concrete, a wood deck can soften and vary the look.

DESIGN AND MATERIALS

A well-designed deck design features lumber, hardware, and accessories made to withstand the outdoor environment. Granted, a deck's lifespan might be limited to 20 or 30 years in a harsh climate, but for most people that's plenty, and even masonry structures suffer some degradation over time.

Mixing masonry and wood structures doesn't complicate the design of an outdoor kitchen, but it often dictates a strict construction sequence. The tile-wrapped grill station here is better suited as a structural core than as an add-on to an existing deck, so it should come first. It provides a solid foundation for the deck frame instead of a burdensome load. The lower base of the grill island is built with a wider, 8-inch block than the upper portion, which features 6-inch block. The 2-inch offset creates a support ledge for the deck frame, a much stronger option than relying on hardware to carry the load. Anchor bolts keep the deck frame from shifting, but they won't be supporting its weight.

An existing deck structure or one built to cook and eat on can be an ideal location for an outdoor kitchen.

Pressure-treated southern yellow pine, the standard lumber for deck frames, should be used for the posts, beams, and other structural members of this project to ensure longevity and rot-resistance.

The deck planking itself can vary from treated pine to any number of engineered or composite products. If you're concerned about having a flammable surface surrounding the grill island, steer clear of cedar decking. Although it's normally an excellent wood for outdoor use, including deck planking, cedar ignites and burns faster than many other woods.

As an alternate consider Ipe, a dense tropical species used for decking that is extremely fire-resistant. Ipe is so hard, however, that it can be difficult to work: It dulls tools quickly and can require the drilling and countersinking of screw holes—operations that can add considerable time to a deck-building project. Engineered decking materials and composite wood products are also good alternatives: They have good fire resistance and are easy to work. Some manufacturers make fire-resistant synthetic pads designed to provide an easy-to-clean, nonflammable surface where grills are used; these are also worth considering

Whatever materials you use, leave gaps between the deck planks and the masonry base to allow water to drain freely. The same holds true when connecting the deck frame to the concrete block base. Use shims and washers as shown to create drainage gaps.

WOOD DECK INSTALLED AROUND A GRILL ISLAND

The trick is to use the grill island as a support for the deck rather than vice-versa. Here's the anatomy:

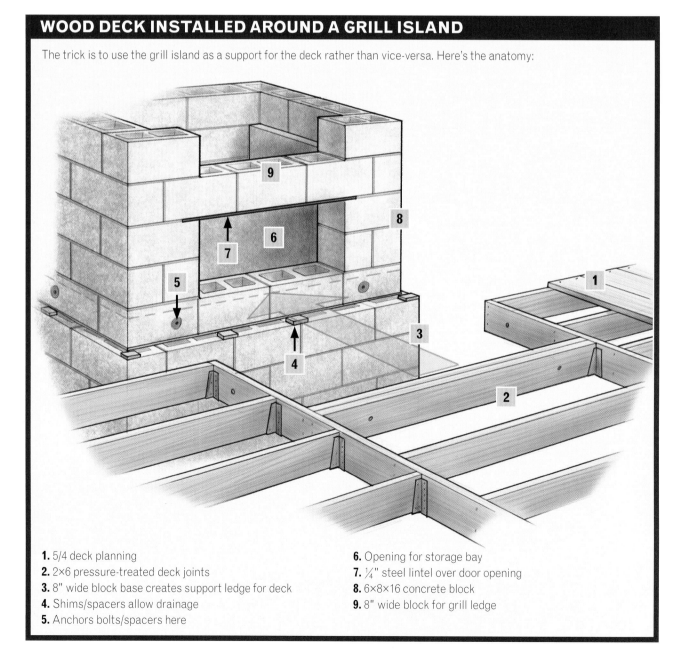

1. 5/4 deck planning
2. 2×6 pressure-treated deck joists
3. 8" wide block base creates support ledge for deck
4. Shims/spacers allow drainage
5. Anchors bolts/spacers here
6. Opening for storage bay
7. $\frac{1}{4}$" steel lintel over door opening
8. 6×8×16 concrete block
9. 8" wide block for grill ledge

RETROFITTING AN EXISTING DECK

This project design calls for constructing the concrete-block grill base first to support the surrounding deck frame. Retrofitting an existing deck with a built-in gas grill island is a common and achievable desire.

A contractor first should evaluate the existing deck framework to ensure that it's sound and worth saving. If not, start fresh and put the masonry foundation first. Even if the existing deck foundation is in good shape, it still probably isn't designed to take the substantial weight of a grill island. At least partial rebuilding is probably necessary. Some of the deck planking will have to come off to reinforce the structural parts below. Plan on installing at least two new concrete pier footings, then additional beams or joists directly below the spot where the grill station will rest. A subfloor of one or two layers of ¾-inch pressure-treated plywood should come next. If the grill island will be a woodframe structure like the one on page 101, a single plywood layer probably will suffice. For a concrete-block island, double up the plywood and top it with a sheet of cement backerboard to allow mortaring the block securely.

Because of the weight involved and the option of plumbing a gas line directly to the grill base, run the plans by local building officials and make sure an experienced contractor is doing the work. There may be code restrictions that affect the project, and a contractor may have recommendations to offer.

This desktop outdoor kitchen features composite decking. Although the kitchen grill station and cabinetry forms a U-shape, the construction principles are the same as for a grill island.

Landscaping

When building and furnishing an outdoor room, incorporate as much nature as possible. That's the whole point of being outdoors in the first place.

CONTAINER PLANTS

Container-grown plants are a boon to anyone planning an outdoor kitchen. The combination of pot and plant adds a sculptural quality and softens the hardscape of a kitchen structure. Containers allow you to import plants into areas—patios and decks and on top of counters and walls—where it would otherwise be impossible for them to grow. Pots contain aggressive plants that might take over a garden bed. They also allow you to take delicate ones inside when frost threatens.

Potted plants offer another benefit: flexibility. Change the landscape to suit the season, occasion, use of the space, and even the number of guests you'll be accommodating—all without transplanting.

Use cascading plants or vines to drape over the edge of a shelf or ledge or choose a potted tree to add interest to a featureless wall. Potted shrubs with a vertical shape can function as moveable dividers to create more intimate spaces on a large patio, for example.

It's surprising how many plants are suited to potted life. Annual flowers, bulbs, miniature roses, small shrubs such as azaleas, and even small trees are suitable for container culture. Because plants in pots are more vulnerable to drying and temperature fluctuations and have modest room to grow, they tolerate less neglect than those planted in the ground, so attend to them regularly.

Edibles are especially at home in an outdoor kitchen, whether planted in pots or beds. Such plants include herbs, spices, and edible flowers, and can be as ornamental as they are tasty.

EDIBLES

Edible plants are natural companions to an outdoor kitchen. To make the most of them incorporate the plants into a landscape design so they actually double as ornamentals. Choose edible plants for their color, form, height, texture, and other visual qualities. Select good-looking edible plants and combine them with standard ornamentals, following the basic rules of landscape design.

Many herbs feature aromatic, silvery gray leaves that blend compatibly with green leaved plants. They have a pleasing aroma when warmed by the sun, brushed in passing, or crushed underfoot. Herb flowers often provide a softening effect. Parsley, thyme, sage, rosemary, basil, and oregano are easy to grow and are conveniently harvested.

Vegetables also often have attractive leaves or fruits with color and texture that combine well with ornamentals. Those with delicious leaves may be difficult to include in an edible landscape, because once they are harvested they leave an empty space. A design should allow you to grow lettuce, spinach, and Swiss chard among flowers without leaving nasty gaps after harvest. Fruiting plants, such as eggplant and pepper, remain even after reaping, so they pose fewer placement problems.

Container plants allow you to green up even a barren spot, such as the top of a masonry wall.

Hold the shrubbery! Diverse species of ornamental grasses define the edge of this outdoor kitchen and pool area. Such plants don't need to be trimmed, as shrubs do; just cut back once a year in the early spring.

GRASSES

The streaming leaves of ornamental grasses form fountains that add a restful aspect to an outdoor room. They're particularly good at softening the texture of structures and hardscapes and combine well with just about any type of plant.

Many grasses are green, but some, such as blue wild rye or blue oat grass, are dusky blue or blue-gray. Others, such as Bowles golden grass are shades of golden green. Zebra grass and variegated Japanese silver grass have boldly striped or banded leaves; purple fountain grass bears dusky, reddish purple blades. Grass flowers take on many attractive forms: open sheaves, foxtails, feathery plumes, and bottlebrushes in subtle, earthy colors.

In late autumn, grasses dry into tall sheaves of leaves and seed heads that can stand through the winter. They bleach to soft hues of straw, wheat, and almond, filling the landscape at a time when other perennials have shriveled.

A unique quality of grasses is the sound they bring to the garden. The slightest breeze creates a symphony of rustling sounds as evocative as a babbling brook or lapping waves.

GROUNDCOVERS

Think of a groundcover planting like a carpet in a well-decorated room. Without it the floor would be bare and the setting would look sterile. Trees, shrubs, flowering perennials, and bulbs can grow through most groundcovers—just the way pieces of furniture rest on a rug.

Groundcover is a useful, low-maintenance lawn substitute. It's particularly appropriate for small outdoor kitchen areas because it does not need mowing or trimming. It also works on slopes, where it looks well groomed with little effort. Many groundcovers require less watering and fertilizer than most lawn grasses, and many groundcover plants flourish in sites hostile to lawn grasses—deep shade or hot, dry slopes.

Even in areas where grass would grow well, groundcovers add texture and depth. Some even flower or show berries.

Stow the mower! Groundcover can be just as green as grass, while offering lower maintenance, more texture, and lushness to the greenscape surrounding this outdoor kitchen.

ROCKS

Rocks create naturalistic effects in and around an outdoor kitchen, contributing color, form, and texture that can complement—or contrast—with your kitchen's manufactured and plant elements. Artfully placed rocks are sculptural. If placed in direct sun they absorb radiant heat, sometimes creating a microclimate that can support plants that are normally north of their natural range. Large, flat rocks can offer guests a perch and large, smooth ones can be a warm spot for sunbathing.

Use rocks compatible with the terrain in your area— they'll look more natural there. Select rocks for their shape and color, avoiding soft, sedimentary types that are apt to separate into layers or crumble.

When arranging rocks, consider scale. Have at least one large rock and several smaller ones in each grouping. To make the rock look like a natural outcropping, bury the lower portion in the soil or below the surface of your patio or deck, leaving about three-fourths above ground level.

Small ornamental trees are ideal choices for outdoor kitchens and their surrounds. They remain in scale with the landscape throughout their lifetime, and their shapes, flowers, branches, and bark are bred for beauty.

TREES

Trees bring incomparable beauty to an outdoor room. They create overhead structure to block and frame views of the sky, a neighbor's house, or distant scenery. Their shade can cool patio, cooking, and gathering areas. Their windbreak ability can turn buffeting gusts into gentle breezes. Planted between an outdoor kitchen and the street, they can serve as a living fence, muffling street sounds and providing privacy. Trees also lend scale. Large trees, in particular, bring peace, calm, and permanence to the landscape.

Trees deserve particular attention when planning an outdoor room. Rather than cutting down trees that seem in the way of your plans, select and consider preserving large, attractive specimens and incorporating them into your design. Discuss having smaller trees moved to more suitable locations. In many cases moving a tree is far less expensive than buying one of similar size. Patios and decks can be planned to incorporate existing trees, allowing them to grow up through the pavement or decking, giving the finished design an unusual touch of character.

When planting trees in and around an outdoor kitchen, determine what tree is best for the spot. Too often large trees crowd homes and yards because the person who planted them lacked a clear understanding of their adult size. Be particularly careful with conifers, which normally grow into massive trees that cast dense shade and can engulf a project.

Is it bedrock ledge or an imported boulder? Careful design and ingenious craftsmanship in fitting the hardwood stair treads to the contour of the surrounding rock result in an artfully naturalistic effect.

A tiny featureless backyard was transformed into what now seems more like an expansive room, because of careful design and execution. Foliage is lush but not overbearing and aged brick ties the patio surfaces, pool, tub, surrounds, and walls together with the main structure.

TIGHT-FIT TIPS

If the outdoor kitchen is in tight quarters, such as a small sunken garden or atop a modest deck, there are still ways to embellish the environment with landscaping. Here's how to think small while thinking green:

- Select a theme or style, but keep an eye on the scale of plants.
- Limit the number of plant species so the area doesn't look too busy.
- Make sure plants, accents, steps, walls, and paving look good up close. In a small area, nothing escapes scrutiny.
- Consider how plants and accents will work together. With so few elements, each piece in the mosaic must fit well.
- Visualize a plant's ultimate, mature size before planting.
- Make hardscape surfaces seem less obtrusive by tying them in with the context, style, and materials of the house.
- Select plants, trees, and shrubs requiring little maintenance—varieties that will grow to their full size without continual pruning.
- Include plants with vertical interest and maximize space by growing plants flat against walls and fences. Vines and vertical plantings can soften the harsh lines of walls and privacy fences that often tightly frame small outdoor kitchens.
- Make use of pots, containers, and built-in and freestanding flowerboxes to add interest and soften areas with lots of walls, fences, and hardscape. The containers themselves add color and shape.

VINES

Among the most versatile and underappreciated of plants, vines have special utility in and around the outdoor kitchen. They soften harsh walls, camouflage unattractive board and chain-link fences, and if grown on an overhead structure, create shade and privacy. A vine planted against the sunny side of a lattice-walled pergola can provide considerable cooling shade, for example, while allowing cooling breezes to penetrate. In addition, annual vines such as clematis, which have sparse growth, can be allowed to grow into shrubbery for added dimension and interest.

One of the great advantages of growing vines in and around outdoor kitchens is that they take up little ground space. You can tuck several between shrubs in a foundation planting or mixed border and let them grow up a wall, fence, or trellis to create a vertical effect. In confined areas, a vine provides lovely effects at eye level and overhead while taking up a fraction of the space of a tree or shrub.

A narrow, exposed side yard formerly fit only for a driveway is shaded and softened by overhead vines grown on a now-invisible frame of tightly stretched wires. The vines' rustling leaves add to the atmosphere.

Retaining Wall Planter

Sloped lots are among the most common challenges for backyard hardscaping. Patios and similar features require reasonably flat and level square footage, and some yards must be excavated or terraced to make room.

It's often impractical or necessary to remove an entire slope, just enough soil to clear a modest area immediately behind the house. This handsome terraced yard is one such site. The owners integrated a built-in cooking station with a handsome retaining wall design. The wood shingle facade matches siding and other elements on the home's exterior, but it's paired with a poured-in-place concrete retaining wall with enough strength and durability to hold back tons of soil.

DESIGN AND MATERIALS

Reinforced concrete is a common material in the construction of retaining walls. It is a proven performer

Disguised as a wood-shingled planter, this retaining wall looks inviting and allows for a level patio in a yard that formerly featured a steep slope.

RETAINING WALL FORM DETAILS

With a modicum of extra work, you can make just about any retaining wall an artful part of the landscape. Here are two different approaches:

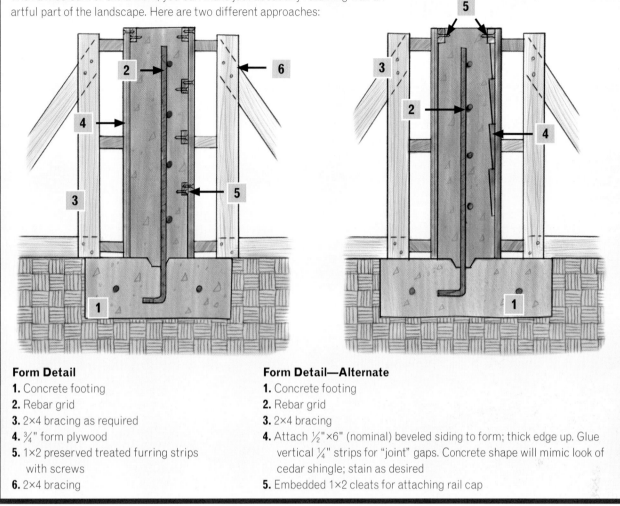

Form Detail

1. Concrete footing
2. Rebar grid
3. 2×4 bracing as required
4. ¾" form plywood
5. 1×2 preserved treated furring strips with screws
6. 2×4 bracing

Form Detail—Alternate

1. Concrete footing
2. Rebar grid
3. 2×4 bracing
4. Attach ½"×6" (nominal) beveled siding to form; thick edge up. Glue vertical ¼" strips for "joint" gaps. Concrete shape will mimic look of cedar shingle; stain as desired
5. Embedded 1×2 cleats for attaching rail cap

and superior to any alternative with similar costs. In this outdoor area the exposed front surface doubles as a graceful aesthetic element that echoes the home's exterior. A straightforward approach might mean installing a conventional concrete wall, then spending a day drilling for anchor bolts to attach wood furring strips to the surface. There is a better way: Instead of blank surfaces on the inside of the plywood concrete forms, these were fitted with pressure-treated 1×2 furring strips attached with short screws. The screws are driven from the outside face of the plywood, so they'll stay accessible for removal. The strips themselves have longer screws that extend into the open area where the concrete will be poured. The strip spacing corresponds to the shingle size and reveal that will be used later.

The forms are braced on top of a concrete footing that has already been excavated and poured as shown. A grid of steel rebar inside will give the wall more strength to resist the soil pressure without cracking or breaking apart.

As the concrete is poured, it surrounds the furring strips and their inward-projecting screws, locking them in place while the concrete hardens and cures. Before the plywood forms are removed, the short screws holding the furring strips are removed. The forms come off, but the wood strips stay embedded in the face of the concrete wall. A second 1×2 strip, called a "stand-off," is fastened to each embedded wood strip, providing a mounting surface for the shingles and creating an air gap for drainage and ventilation.

At the top of the wall, wood strips are embedded in both faces. These provide a mounting surface for a cedar cap rail. With this integral wood framework in place, installing the shingles and trim is easier and faster using conventional methods. If horizontal lap siding were the finished surface, the same method could be used, but the embedded wood strips and the stand-off strips would be oriented vertically like studs in a conventional wall frame.

Cedar shingles have a summer-cottage connotation that works well in outdoor-kitchen settings. Having the flexibility to apply them to masonry walls such as walk-out basement exterior walls broadens their appeal.

Another Way to Get the Look

Although the process of fitting wood strips to be embedded in the concrete wall might seem complex, it's actually a simple technique that saves considerable time when applying shingle siding. It is also possible to have the concrete wall itself mimic that same look right when you pull off the forms. As shown in the Retaining Wall Form Details illustration on page 179, the inside face of the form can be fitted with tapered material such as beveled wood siding. It is installed upside down so it creates the correct taper pattern in the concrete. For an even more realistic look, narrow vertical strips can be glued to the beveled siding to create fine grooves in the concrete face, simulating gaps between shingles. After the concrete is placed and cured and the forms removed, the front surface will feature the same contours common to shingle siding, without having to attach additional materials. A wood-colored concrete stain would give the surface a more authentic look.

A DISGUISED CONCRETE WALL

Cedar shingled concrete? It's as easy as siding a wood wall when you embed furring strips in the pour.

1. Stand off 1×2 furring strips
2. Concrete footing
3. ½" or ¾" steel rebar
4. Embedded/anchored 1×2 furring strips
5. 4" drainage pipe in rock fill
6. Concrete retaining wall with rebar
7. Soil backfill
8. Cedar shingles attach to standoff strips
9. Patio height
10. 2×10 cedar rail cap

Getting It Done

With an overview of the planning process and what it takes to accomplish a variety of different types of outdoor kitchen projects, it's time to make the project a reality. Should it be a do-it-yourself or a contracted project—or both? What types of expert help would benefit the project? What about financing, budgets, and the actual construction process? This chapter points you toward answers for all these questions. Finish reading it and get to work.

Selecting a Pro

Choosing the best professionals to design and build an outdoor kitchen project makes your entire experience more enjoyable and ensures top-notch results. Whether searching for a landscape designer, architect, or contractor, use these tactics to find the best one for you:

• **Gather.** Collect names of professionals to investigate and interview. Ask friends and colleagues for suggestions and recommendations. Identify local referrals with the help of professional organizations, such as the American Institute of Architects, 800/242-3837, aia.org; The National Kitchen and Bath Association, 877/NKBA-PRO or 800/843-6522, nkba.org; the American Society of Landscape Architects, 202/898-2444, asla.org; or the Professional Landcare Network, 800/395-2522, landcarenetwork.org.

• **Explore.** Call the professionals on your list—you should have at least four to six from each profession you plan to use—and ask for references. Then contact the people they name and ask them to recount their positive and negative experiences. Also ask for a couple of projects that are currently underway and talk to those homeowners.

• **Evaluate.** Based on these references, interview the top three professionals in each category and look at their finished projects. Savvy architects, designers, and contractors will ask you questions to determine your expectations and needs. You should come away from each interview and tour with an idea of the quality of their work and how well your personalities and visions for the project match.

• **Solicit.** To narrow your choices to between two or more architects or landscape designers, it may be worth the additional cost to solicit preliminary drawings from each one. This is a great way to test your working relationship.

• **Request bids**. If there are specific appliances or features that you want to include in your outdoor kitchen, list them and give the list to the bidding contractors. Three weeks is a reasonable amount of time for each of them to get back to you with a bid. When bids return, study them for the following: specific, itemized materials lists; a schedule noting what will be done when; when payments will be made based on that progress; and the contractor's fee. Bid prices are not necessarily predictors of work quality, so ask contractors to explain their bids in detail.

• **Weigh the criteria.** Don't base your final decision on which professional to use on cost alone. Instead weigh what you learned in the interview with the thoroughness of the bid itself.

As a general rule, the smaller the space, the more your project will benefit from the services of an architect, landscape designer, or both. They can make the most of a diminutive yard such as this one.

A small deck can be a do-it-yourself job, but if an outdoor kitchen involves a large, multilevel project like this one, working with contractors who specialize in decks makes sense. They'll have the material, design, and engineering expertise to create a robust and good-looking structure.

Sometimes it pays to start small and add on to a kitchen as a budget allows. A premium stand-alone grill and a well-constructed, well-landscaped patio are great places to start.

Controlling Costs

If your plans and projects are bigger than your billfold, use these tips to save dollars:

• **Choose materials wisely.** For example, concrete patio surfaces cost far less than stone tile and can be customized with stains and molds to look much like the real thing.

• **Get help.** Swap jobs with handy neighbors. Throw a theme party and feed guests. Ask family and friends to help.

• **Assist as a general laborer.** Consider clearing or preparing the site, doing daily site cleanup, or acting as a helper or gofer for your contractor. A contract that specifies cost plus fixed fees credits your labor against a contractor's fee.

• **Act as your own general contractor.** This is a full-time job and not a task for the faint of heart. You need to understand the project and the order of work and have a thorough knowledge of building codes.

• **Rent or buy any equipment needed.** Buying equipment often costs more than renting it if you are doing anything yourself.

• **Build your project in stages.** Start with the basics, then add amenities as time and budget allows. This approach has many benefits: You can enjoy your outdoor kitchen right away. As you enjoy using it, your experience can help you adopt your plans. Staging the job may enable paying for it out of savings, avoiding debt and interest costs.

PREPARING YOUR OWN ESTIMATE

If you'll be doing most of the work yourself, figure costs by breaking the work into manageable chunks. Rather than shopping for the best prices on individual items, find a home center or lumber source that offers reasonable prices and top-notch service. You'll save yourself time and hassle by getting to know the sales staff at your chosen store. Make a habit of visiting when the store's not busy and share your plans with the staff—they can become invaluable partners in estimating what each phase of a project will cost.

BE READY FOR THE 10-15% RULE

No matter how carefully you or your contractor(s) prepare bids, savvy homeowners know that a remodeling project generally ends up costing 10-15 percent or more than estimated. Unexpected situations and changes are commonplace. Once you get started, enthusiastic homeowners often upgrade plans and materials, figuring, "As long as we've gone to this much trouble, let's go further." Spare yourself hassle and headache by anticipating such budget overruns.

An existing deck and a portable lawn shelter can serve as a great springboard for a pay-as-you-go outdoor kitchen project. Working in stages, you can add cooking equipment, lighting, a seating area, and perhaps a fireplace or water feature—all without breaking the budget.

Finding the Money

You have a wide choice of ways to pay for a new outdoor kitchen:

• **With savings.** If you've socked away enough to fund your project, you're sitting pretty: no waiting, no finance costs, no payments to make.

• **With income.** By doing a project in stages, you can put time on your side, and pay for (and complete) a portion of the work over a set schedule. This is another way to avoid finance costs. By stretching out the project, you also have more time to shop for bargains on big-ticket elements, such as appliances, and to do some or all of the work yourself. On the other hand, this prolongs the process and delays the result.

• **With a home equity loan.** If you have enough equity in your home to pay for the outdoor kitchen you want, you may be able to finance the project with a lump-sum home equity loan. If you don't have enough savings to fund your project and you don't like the inconvenience of paying as you go, such a loan can be an attractive alternative. Interest on home equity loans is often tax deductible and rates are generally lower than for consumer loans.

• **With a home equity line of credit.** Get a home equity line of credit. Such a loan allows you to borrow up to a preset amount on a revolving credit account that works similarly to a credit card, generally with lower rates and tax-deductible interest. The advantage over the lump-sum loan is that you pay interest only on money as you spend it. Since the cost of remodeling is spread over time as you buy materials and pay contractors, the interest costs for a line of credit will be less than for a lump-sum loan, all other factors being equal.

• **With a mortgage.** If you're planning to remodel a home that you're about to buy, ask your lender about the possibility of getting a mortgage for the price of the home plus the price of the remodeling you seek. The interest will be tax-deductible and the cost spread out over the term of the loan, making this a relatively painless and money-savvy option.

Compared with a wood-fired oven or masonry fireplace and chimney, a fire pit is a relatively inexpensive way to add some heat, light, and campfire ambiance to your outdoor kitchen.

Major outdoor projects such as this kitchen, dining area, hot tub, and pool can be just as costly and complex as adding a substantial new wing to your home. They require similarly detailed planning, coordinating, and budgeting. The result, however, can put a private resort in your backyard.

• **With a credit card.** This is generally the funding source of last resort due to high interest rates. This method can be useful if, for example, you're taking advantage of a low "teaser" interest rate, need to borrow a relatively small amount, and/or can pay off your balance quickly. Be careful, though, because a combination of cost overruns, job delays, and teaser rate expiration dates can leave you with a big, high-interest balance to pay.

• **With a combination of sources.** Sometimes a patchwork of funding from a variety of sources is the way to go: you might have some savings, pay some as you go, pay for appliances with a special, no-interest-for-a-year retailer's promotion, and contribute some sweat equity.

THE CONTRACT

Bids are in; you've chosen your contractor(s). Protect everyone with a written contract that includes these features:

• **Detailed description of work** that will be done by the contractor, subcontractor, and you. This should include demolition and construction.

• **Schedule of work** that also describes how delays will be handled and when payments will be made.

• **Complete description of materials.**

• **Protective elements** include a right of recision clause giving you a short period of time to back out of the project, proof of bonding, and an insurance certificate, a warranty guaranteeing work and materials for at least one year, and mechanic's lien waivers. The latter protects you from having a lien placed against your property if your contractor doesn't pay his or her subcontractors.

• **Statements specifying responsibilities** as to who will secure building permits and arrange inspections.

• **A statement of how change orders**—modifications or additions to planned work—will be handled.

• **A final walkthrough and approval** that precedes final payment. It's best to allow a couple of days after construction is complete to conduct the walkthrough, when you'll need to point out anything that is not to your satisfaction. The contract should allow the contractor a reasonable amount of time to remedy unsatisfactory situations.

STAGES AND PHASES

Prepare for an outdoor kitchen project by knowing what to expect and how to save money. Follow these steps:

• **Plan.** Determine whether you'll use a design professional, pin down the design, and begin shaping the budget. When shopping, ask how long it will take to receive materials once ordered. Build these time lags into the schedule. Meet with local building code officials to see if you need a building permit and to make sure your project won't violate any zoning restrictions.

• **Confer.** Invite key players to your home including the architect or designer, contractor, primary subcontractors, and the job supervisor. Review project particulars and establish ground rules between you and the professionals you hire. You need an especially good communication plan. One option is to place a notebook in a prominent location. This is where both you and the crew can jot down comments and questions.

Any contract for outdoor living areas should specify the quality and type of materials used, the responsibilities of the various contractors and other professionals involved in the job, and a detailed description and schedule of the work to be performed.

- **Construct.**
- **Finish.** Walk through the completed project with your contractor and architect, noting any concerns or unfinished details. The contractor follows up on your list in order to complete the project.

BUILDER

A contractor is responsible for turning plans into your finished outdoor kitchen. A good contractor will:
- **Serve as part of the initial team**, providing a craftsman's insight into the execution of a design in the most workmanlike, cost-efficient manner possible.
- **Select the best subcontractors** in your area to execute your design.
- **Schedule the work** to ensure that the job flows sequentially, that materials are available as they are needed, and that coordination between the various trades on the job runs smoothly.
- **Supervise the job** to make sure the blueprints are interpreted correctly and that workmanship is high quality.
- **Communicate with the architect and homeowner**, keeping them informed of how the project is proceeding and involving them in decisions that need to be made as work progresses.

YOUR ROLE

As client, you're the project's parent—your needs, wants, and desires are its reason for being, and your taste and decisions shape its development. Here are some tips to help the process go smoothly:
- **Do your homework.** Before commissioning your outdoor kitchen, review the kitchens depicted in this book one more time, looking for features and elements to include.
- **Be thoughtful and open to ideas.** When working with professionals, it doesn't pay be an autocratic know-it-all who demands that everything be done exactly to your every whim. Such an attitude rules out the better results of the collaboration of a dedicated team, and it usually increases costs and earns you the Client-from-the-Underworld award from your architect, landscape architect, and contractor. Your team will be much more likely to go the extra mile for you if you develop a good relationship by listening and cooperating with them.
- **Be decisive when necessary.** Take on some of the responsibility yourself. You'll be called upon to make lots of choices throughout the process.
- **Communicate clearly.** The outdoor kitchen that gets built is the one that gets communicated, detail by detail, to the designer and builder. Be as clear, concise, direct,

A well-planned project is an efficient project. Here a designer sketches a concept for a wood-fired oven, hearth, and chimney located on a second-floor deck.

and articulate as possible when discussing your project with the team. Make notes of points to mention before meetings and refer to them during discussions. Take notes of decisions you need to relay back to your team, and recognize when your language becomes vague or noncommittal—that generally means you're not clear in your own mind about what you want. Tell your team you'll think about the issue and contact them soon rather than leave them with ambiguous feedback. If you're part of a couple, designate one go-to person. That person can take down information, talk to the spouse, and respond to the team. Such an arrangement prevents a builder, for example, from hearing conflicting responses from each owner.
- **Be flexible and realistic.** Remember that the rest of the team—like you—are fallible human beings. They'll make mistakes. Weather, materials, supplier problems, permits, and other details may and probably will conspire to delay a project, increase its cost, or cause it to evolve in unforeseen ways. An ability to take the unexpected in stride and respond with good humor and a problem-solving attitude can help make your project successful and enjoyable.

8

Favorite

Now that the outdoor kitchen is ready to go, it's time to fire up the grill (or smoker, or rotisserie, or wood-fired oven) and make some mouth-watering meals—the kind only made outdoors! This chapter features delicious recipes from the renowned Better Homes and Gardens® Test Kitchen. Each recipe has been tested to perfection and results are guaranteed every time you prepare any of these sizzling dishes.

Grilling Recipes

Texas-Style Beef Ribs

Three-Way Chicken Wings

Prep: 10 minutes   **Grill:** 25 minutes

24   chicken wings (about 4 pounds)

1. Prepare desired sauce(s). Set aside. Rinse chicken wings; pat dry with paper towels. If desired, cut off and discard wing tips from chicken wings.

2. For a charcoal grill, arrange medium-hot coals around a drip pan. Test for medium heat above pan. Pour 1 inch of water into pan. Place chicken wings on a lightly greased grill rack over drip pan. Cover; grill for 25 to 30 minutes or until chicken is tender and juices run clear, turning once and brushing occasionally with some of desired sauce(s) during the last 5 minutes of grilling. (For a gas grill, preheat grill. Reduce heat to medium. Adjust for indirect cooking. Grill as above.)

3. To serve, reheat the remaining sauce(s). Transfer to a serving bowl or bowls and use as dipping sauces for the grilled wings. Makes 24 wings.

Easy Barbecue Sauce: In a small saucepan stir together 1 cup bottled chili sauce, ½ cup currant jelly, 2 tablespoons snipped fresh chives, and 2 teaspoons yellow mustard. Cook and stir until jelly is melted. Makes about 1½ cups.

Spicy Mustard Sauce: In a small saucepan stir together 1⅓ cups chicken broth, ½ cup hot-style mustard, 4 teaspoons cornstarch, 2 teaspoons soy sauce, and if desired, a few dashes bottled hot pepper sauce. Cook and stir until thickened and bubbly. Cook and stir for 2 minutes more. Makes about 1¾ cups.

Sweet-and-Sour Sauce: In a small saucepan stir together ⅔ cup unsweetened pineapple juice, ⅔ cup red wine vinegar, ½ cup packed brown sugar, 2 tablespoons cornstarch, 2 tablespoons soy sauce, and ¼ teaspoon ground ginger. Cook and stir until thickened and bubbly. Cook and stir for 2 minutes more. Makes about 1⅔ cups.

Nutrition facts per wing: 71 cal., 2 g total fat (0 g sat. fat), 18 mg chol., 180 mg sodium, 7 g carbo., 0 g fiber, 7 g pro.

Texas-Style Beef Ribs

Prep: 25 minutes   Grill: 1 hour

3	to 4 pounds beef back ribs (about 8 ribs)
1	teaspoon salt
1	teaspoon black pepper
1	large onion, finely chopped (1 cup)
½	cup honey
½	cup ketchup
1	4-ounce can diced green chile peppers, drained
1	tablespoon chili powder
1	clove garlic, minced
½	teaspoon dry mustard

1. Trim fat from ribs. Cut into serving size pieces. Sprinkle both sides of meat with salt and pepper; rub in with your fingers.

2. For a charcoal grill, arrange medium-hot coals around a drip pan. Test for medium heat above pan. Pour 1 inch of water into pan. Place ribs on grill rack directly over drip pan. (Or place ribs in a rib rack and place on grill rack.) Cover; grill for 1 to 1½ hours or until the ribs are tender. Add more coals as necessary. (For a gas grill, preheat grill. Reduce heat to medium. Adjust for indirect cooking. Cover; grill as above.)

3. Meanwhile, for sauce, in a small saucepan stir together onion, honey, ketchup, chile peppers, chili powder, garlic, and dry mustard. Cook and stir over low heat 10 minutes. About 10 minutes before the ribs are finished grilling, brush sauce generously over ribs. Continue grilling until glazed. Pass remaining sauce. Makes 4 servings.

Nutrition facts per serving: 403 cal., 12 g total fat (5 g sat. fat), 79 mg chol., 1,125 mg sodium, 49 g carbo., 2 g fiber, 26 g pro.

Garden-Stuffed Fish Steaks

Garden-Stuffed Fish Steaks

Prep: 25 minutes   Grill: 14 minutes

4	5- to 6-ounce fresh or frozen swordfish or tuna steaks, 1 inch thick
½	cup coarsely shredded carrot
¼	cup sliced green onion (2)
1	clove garlic, minced
2	tablespoons butter or margarine
1	small tomato, seeded and chopped (½ cup)
2	tablespoons fine dry seasoned bread crumbs
2	tablespoons grated Parmesan cheese

1. Thaw fish, if frozen. Rinse fish; pat dry with paper towels. Make a pocket in each steak by cutting horizontally from one side almost through to the other side. Cover; chill until ready to grill.

2. For stuffing, in small saucepan cook carrot, green onion, and garlic in hot butter until vegetables are tender. Remove from heat. Add tomato, bread crumbs, and cheese; toss lightly to mix. Spoon about ¼ cup stuffing into each pocket. Secure the openings with wooden toothpicks.

3. For a charcoal grill, grill fish on the greased rack of an uncovered grill directly over medium-hot coals for 14 to 18 minutes or until fish flakes easily when tested with a fork, gently turning once halfway through grilling. (For a gas grill, preheat grill. Reduce heat to medium-hot. Place fish on greased grill rack over heat. Cover; grill as above.) Makes 4 servings.

Nutrition facts per serving: 293 cal., 16 g total fat (4 g sat. fat), 58 mg chol., 352 mg sodium, 5 g carbo., 1 g fiber, 30 g pro.

Smoked Portobello and Walnut Pasta

Soak: 1 hour Prep: 20 minutes Grill: 30 minutes.

4 to 6 hickory wood chunks or 4 cups hickory wood chips
3 tablespoons olive oil
2 tablespoons white wine vinegar
1 tablespoon snipped fresh tarragon or 1 teaspoon dried tarragon, crushed
1 tablespoon snipped fresh thyme or 1 teaspoon dried thyme, crushed
2 cloves garlic, minced
½ teaspoon black pepper
¼ teaspoon salt
8 ounces fresh portobello mushrooms
2 medium zucchini, halved lengthwise
2 medium red sweet peppers, halved lengthwise, or 4 roma tomatoes, halved lengthwise and seeded
¾ cup walnut pieces
2 cups packaged dried bow tie pasta (about 6 ounces)
½ cup finely shredded Parmesan cheese (2 ounces) or 1 cup crumbled feta cheese
¼ cup fresh basil, cut into thin strips

1. At least 1 hour before grilling, soak wood chunks in enough water to cover. For dressing, in a small bowl combine olive oil, vinegar, tarragon, thyme, garlic, black pepper, and salt; set aside. Cut off mushroom stems even with caps; discard stems. Lightly rinse mushroom caps and gently pat dry with paper towels.

2. Drain wood chunks. For a charcoal grill, arrange medium-hot coals around a drip pan. Test for medium heat above pan. Sprinkle drained wood chunks over coals. Pour 1 inch of water into pan. Place mushrooms, zucchini, and sweet peppers on lightly greased grill rack over drip pan; brush with some of the dressing. Place walnuts on a piece of heavy foil; add to grill. Cover and grill 15 minutes. Remove walnuts from grill. Turn vegetables; brush with remaining dressing. Cover and grill about 15 minutes more or until peppers are crisp-tender and mushrooms are tender. (For a gas grill, preheat grill. Reduce heat to medium. Adjust for indirect cooking. Add wood chips according to manufacturer's directions. Grill as above.)

3. Meanwhile, cook pasta according to package directions; drain. Return pasta to hot pan. Cut vegetables into bite-size pieces. Add grilled vegetables, walnuts, cheese, and basil to cooked pasta; toss to combine. Serve immediately. Makes 6 side-dish servings.

Nutrition facts per serving: 316 cal., 20 g total fat (2 g sat. fat), 31 mg chol., 205 mg sodium, 27 g carbo., 3 g fiber, 11 g pro.

Smoked Portobello and Walnut Pasta

Caribbean Chops with Mango Sauce

Memphis-Style Smoked Pork with Bourbon Sauce

Prep: 25 minutes   Marinate: 24 hours   Soak: 1 hour
Smoke: 4 hours   Stand: 15 minutes

- 1   8-ounce can tomato sauce
- 1   cup chopped onion (1 large)
- 1   cup cider vinegar
- ½   cup bourbon or beef broth
- ¼   cup Worcestershire sauce
- 2   tablespoons brown sugar
- ¼   teaspoon black pepper
       Dash bottled hot pepper sauce
- 1   4 ½- to 5-pound boneless pork shoulder roast
- 8   to 10 hickory wood chunks

1. For sauce, in a medium saucepan combine tomato sauce, onion, ½ cup of the vinegar, the bourbon, Worcestershire sauce, brown sugar, black pepper, and hot pepper sauce. Bring to boiling; reduce heat. Simmer, covered, for 15 minutes; cool. Reserve 1 cup of sauce; cover reserved sauce and chill until ready to serve.
2. Meanwhile, trim fat from meat. Place meat in a resealable plastic bag set in a shallow dish. For marinade, combine the remaining sauce and the remaining vinegar. Pour over meat; seal bag. Marinade in the refrigerator for 24 hours, turning bag occasionally. Drain meat, reserving marinade.
3. At least 1 hour before smoke-cooking, soak wood chunks in enough water to cover.
4. Drain wood chunks. In a smoker arrange preheated coals, half of the drained wood chunks, and water pan according to the manufacturer's directions. Pour water into pan. Place meat on grill rack over pan. Cover and smoke for 4 to 5 hours or until meat is tender, basting occasionally with marinade during the first

Memphis-Style Smoked Pork with Bourbon Sauce

3 hours of smoking. Add additional coals, wood chunks, and water as needed to maintain temperature and moisture. Remove meat from smoker.
5. Cover meat with foil; let stand 15 minutes before carving. Meanwhile, in a small saucepan cook the reserved 1 cup sauce over medium heat until heated through. Slice meat. Serve meat with sauce. Makes 12 servings.
Nutrition facts per serving: 354 cal., 17 g total fat (6 g sat. fat), 112 mg chol., 253 mg sodium, 6 g carbo., 0 g fiber, 30 g pro.

Caribbean Chops with Mango Sauce

Soak: 1 hour   Prep: 20 minutes   Smoke: 1¾ hours

- 6   to 9 apple or cherry wood chunks or 3 cups wood chips
- 4   pork loins, cut 1½ inches thick (about 2½ pounds total)
- 2   to 3 teaspoons Jamaican jerk seasoning
- 1   medium mango, peeled, seeded, and finely chopped (about 1 cup)
- ¼   cup sliced green onion (2)
- 2   tablespoons snipped fresh cilantro or snipped fresh parsley
- ½   teaspoon finely shredded orange peel
- 2   teaspoons orange juice
- ¼   teaspoon Jamaican jerk seasoning

1. At least 1 hour before smoking, soak the wood chunks or chips in enough water to cover. Drain before using.
2. Trim fat from chops. Sprinkle the 2 teaspoons jerk seasoning evenly over chops; rub in with your fingers.
3. In a smoker arrange preheated coals, drained wood chunks, and water pan according to the manufacturer's directions. Pour water into pan. Place chops on the grill rack over water pan. Cover;

smoke for 1¾ hours to 2¼ hours or until juices run clear (160°F). Add additional coals and water as needed to maintain temperature and moisture.
4. Meanwhile, for sauce in a medium mixing bowl stir together mango, green onion, cilantro, orange peel, orange juice, and the ¼ teaspoon jerk seasoning. Let stand at room temperature for 15 to 20 minutes for flavors to blend. Serve sauce over chops. Makes 4 servings.

Grill method: Drain wood chips. In a grill with a cover arrange preheated coals around a drip pan. Test for medium heat above pan. Sprinkle half of the drained chips over the coals. Pour 1 inch of water into pan. Place chops on the grill rack directly over the drip pan. Cover and grill chops for 35 to 40 minutes or until juices run clear. Add additional wood chips every 15 minutes.
Nutrition facts per serving: 347 cal., 11 g total fat (4 g sat. fat), 138 mg chol., 224 mg sodium, 11 g carbo., 1 g fiber, 49 g pro.

Smoky Fajitas

Prep: 30 minutes   **Marinate:** 6 hours   **Soak:** 1 hour   **Grill:** 23 minutes

1	1- to 1¼ pound beef flank steak
1	cup beer
½	cup lime juice
½	cup chopped onion (1 medium)
3	tablespoons cooking oil
2	tablespoons bottled steak sauce
1	tablespoon chili powder
1	teaspoon ground cumin
4	cloves garlic, minced
1	bay leaf
2	cups oak or hickory wood chips
3	large red, yellow, and/or green sweet peppers, cut into thin strips (3 cups)
1	large onion, thinly sliced (1 cup)
8	7-inch flour or corn tortillas
1	recipe Pico de Gallo

1. Score both sides of steak in a diamond pattern by making shallow diagonal cuts at 1-inch intervals. Place steak in a resealable plastic bag set in a shallow dish. For marinade, in a medium bowl combine beer, lime juice, the ½ cup chopped onion, the oil, steak sauce, chili powder, cumin, and garlic. Pour over steak. Seal bag; turn to coat steak. Marinate in the refrigerator for at least 6 hours or up to 24 hours, turning bag occasionally.

2. At least 1 hour before cooking, soak wood chips in enough water to cover.

3. Fold a 24×18-inch piece of heavy foil in half to make a 12×18-inch rectangle. Place pepper strips and sliced onion in center of foil. Bring up two opposite edges of foil and seal with a double fold. Fold remaining ends to completely enclose vegetables, leaving space for steam to build. Fold a 42×18-inch piece of heavy foil in half to make a 21×18-inch rectangle. Place tortillas in center of foil. Bring up two opposite edges of the foil; fold remaining ends to completely enclose the tortillas.

4. For a charcoal grill, arrange medium-hot coals around a drip pan. Test for medium heat above pan. Sprinkle drained wood chips over coals. Pour 1 inch water into pan. Drain steak, discarding marinade. Place steak on grill rack directly over drip pan. Place pepper packet on grill rack directly over coals. Cover and grill for 23 to 28 minutes or until steak is medium doneness (160°F) and vegetables are tender. Place tortilla packet on grill rack directly over coals for the last 10 minutes of grilling. (For a gas grill, preheat grill. Reduce heat to medium. Add drained wood chips according to manufacturer's directions. Adjust for indirect cooking. Place steak and pepper packet, then tortilla packet on grill rack and grill as above.)

5. To serve, thinly slice steak diagonally across the grain. Divide steak and pepper mixture among the tortillas. Roll up and serve with Pico de Gallo. Makes 4 servings.

Pico de Gallo: In a medium bowl stir together 2 roma tomatoes, chopped; 2 green onions, sliced; 1 fresh serrano chile pepper, seeded and chopped (see note, below); 2 tablespoons snipped fresh cilantro; and ⅛ teaspoon salt. Cover; refrigerate up to 24 hours.

Note: Because hot chile peppers contain volatile oils that can burn your skin and eyes, avoid direct contact with chiles as much as possible. When working with chile peppers, wear plastic or rubber gloves. If your bare hands do touch the chile peppers, wash your hands well with soap and water

Nutrition facts per serving: 425 cal., 15 g total fat (5 g sat. fat), 46 mg chol., 405 mg sodium, 42 g carbo., 4 g fiber, 31 g pro.

Smoky Fajitas

Honey-Soy Grilled Chicken

Prep: 15 minutes   Marinate: 6 hours   Grill: 1¼ hours   Stand: 10 minutes

1	3- to 4-pound whole broiler-fryer chicken
¼	cup water
¼	cup soy sauce
¼	cup dry sherry
1	green onion, sliced (⅛ cup)
2	cloves garlic, minced
½	teaspoon five-spice powder
1	tablespoon cooking oil
1	tablespoon honey

1. Remove the neck and giblets from chicken. Skewer the neck skin to the back. Twist wing tips under back. Tie legs to tail with 100-percent-cotton string. Place chicken in a resealable plastic bag set in a deep bowl.

2. For marinade, in a small bowl combine water, soy sauce, sherry, green onion, garlic, and five-spice powder. Pour over chicken; seal bag. Marinate in the refrigerator for 6 to 24 hours, turning bag occasionally. Drain chicken, discarding marinade. Brush chicken with oil.

3. For a charcoal grill, arrange medium-hot coals around a drip pan. Test for medium heat above the pan. Pour 1 inch water into drip pan. Place chicken, breast side up, on grill rack over drip pan. Cover; grill for 1¼ to 1¾ hours or until chicken is no longer pink and drumsticks move easily (180°F in thigh muscle), brushing with honey during the last 10 minutes of grilling. (For a gas grill, preheat grill. Reduce heat to medium. Adjust for indirect cooking. Grill as above, except place chicken on a rack in a roasting pan.)

4. Remove chicken from grill. Cover with foil; let stand 10 minutes before carving. Makes 4 to 6 servings.

Nutrition facts per serving: 251 cal., 14 g total fat (4 g sat. fat), 79 mg chol., 245 mg sodium, 3 g carbo., 0 g fiber, 25 g pro.

Greek Lamb Platter

Prep: 20 minutes   Marinate: 8 hours   Grill: 8 minutes

1½   **pounds boneless leg of lamb**
1   **tablespoon finely shredded lemon peel**
⅔   **cup lemon juice**
6   **tablespoons olive oil**
⅓   **cup snipped fresh oregano**
½   **teaspoon salt**
⅛   **teaspoon black pepper**
½   **cup snipped fresh parsley**
2   **ounces crumbled feta cheese (½ cup)**
¼   **cup pitted, sliced kalamata olives or other ripe olives**
¼   **teaspoon ground cinnamon**
¼   **teaspoon black pepper**
2   **pounds roma tomatoes (about 3 cups)**

1. Trim fat from meat. Cut meat across the grain into ½- to ¾-inch slices. Place meat in a large resealable plastic bag set in a shallow dish. For marinade, in a small bowl stir together lemon peel, ⅓ cup of the lemon juice, 4 tablespoons of the oil, the oregano, salt, and the ⅛ teaspoon pepper. Pour marinade over lamb; seal bag. Marinate in the refrigerator for 8 to 24 hours, turning bag occasionally.

2. In a large bowl combine the remaining lemon juice, 1 tablespoon of the remaining oil, the parsley, feta cheese, olives, cinnamon, and the ¼ teaspoon pepper; set aside. Drain meat, discarding marinade. Brush tomatoes with the remaining 1 tablespoon oil.

3. For a charcoal grill, grill meat and tomatoes on the rack of an uncovered grill directly over medium coals until meat is desired doneness and tomatoes are slightly charred, turning once halfway through grilling. Allow about 8 minutes for medium-rare (145°F) or about 10 minutes for medium doneness (160°F). (For a gas grill, preheat grill. Reduce heat to medium. Place meat and tomatoes on grill rack over heat. Cover and grill as above.)

4. Transfer tomatoes to a cutting board; cool slightly and slice. Toss the tomatoes with the feta cheese mixture. Serve meat with tomato mixture. Makes 6 servings.

Nutrition facts per serving: 256 cal., 14 g total fat (4 g sat. fat), 66 mg chol., 493 mg sodium, 11 g carbo., 0 g fiber, 22 g pro.

Greek Lamb Platter

Middle Eastern-Style Pizza

Nectarine Sundaes

Prep: 10 minutes   Grill: 10 minutes

- 2 medium nectarines, halved lengthwise and pitted
- 1 tablespoon butter or margarine, melted
- 2 tablespoons honey
- ⅛ teaspoon ground nutmeg
- ½ pint (1 cup) vanilla ice cream
- 1 cup blueberries
- 1 cup sliced strawberries
- ¼ cup crushed amaretti cookies, crushed gingersnaps, or granola

1. Brush cut sides of nectarines with butter.
2. For a charcoal grill, grill nectarines on the rack of an uncovered grill directly over medium coals for 10 to 12 minutes or until tender, turning and brushing once with honey halfway through grilling. (For a gas grill, preheat grill. Reduce heat to medium. Place nectarines on grill rack over heat. Cover; grill as above.)
3. To serve, sprinkle cut sides of nectarines with nutmeg. Place in dessert dishes, cut sides up. Top each nectarine half with some of the ice cream, blueberries, and strawberries. Sprinkle with crushed cookies. Makes 4 servings.
Nutrition facts per serving: 212 cal., 7 g total fat (3 g sat. fat), 15 mg chol., 93 mg sodium, 36 g carbo., 2 g fiber, 2 g pro.

Middle Eastern-Style Pizza

Prep: 15 minutes   Grill: 13 minutes

- 12 ounces ground lamb or ground beef
- 1 8-ounce can tomato sauce
- 1 clove garlic, minced
- ¼ teaspoon allspice
  Nonstick cooking spray
- 1 10-ounce package refrigerated pizza dough
- 2 roma tomatoes, thinly sliced
- ½ cup chopped green sweet pepper (1 medium)
- ¼ cup minced fresh mint
- 1 tablespoon pine nuts, toasted*
- ½ cup crumbled feta cheese (2 ounces) (optional)
  Plain low-fat yogurt (optional)

1. For sauce, in a large skillet cook ground lamb over medium heat until meat is no longer pink; drain well. Stir in tomato sauce, garlic, and allspice; set aside.
2. Lightly coat a 12-inch pizza pan with nonstick cooking spray. With your fingers, pat the pizza dough onto the prepared pan.
3. For a charcoal grill, grill pizza crust in pan on the rack of an uncovered grill directly over medium coals for 5 minutes. (For a gas grill, preheat grill. Reduce heat to medium. Place pizza crust in pan on grill rack over heat. Cover and grill as above.) Carefully remove pizza crust from the grill.
4. Turn crust; spread with sauce. Top with tomatoes and sweet pepper. Return pizza to grill. Cover and grill for 8 to 10 minutes more or until pizza is heated through, checking occasionally to make sure the crust doesn't overbrown. Remove pizza from grill.
5. Sprinkle with mint, pine nuts, and if desired, feta cheese. If desired, top with yogurt. Makes 4 servings.
*Note: To toast nuts, spread in a single layer in a shallow baking pan. Bake in a 350°F oven for 5 to 10 minutes or until light brown, watching carefully and stirring once or twice.
Nutrition facts per serving: 388 cal., 16 g total fat (5 g sat. fat), 57 mg chol., 784 mg sodium, 40 g carbo., 2 g fiber, 22 g pro.

Nectarine Sundaes

Glossary

A-B

Actual dimension True size of a piece of lumber.

Aggregate The noncement solids used to make concrete. Crushed rock is the coarse aggregate; sand is the fine aggregate.

Backerboard A ready-made panel made with nylon mesh and a cement or gypsum core; used as a substrate for ceramic tile installations.

Backsplash The area directly above and behind a countertop. A backsplash can be an integral part of the countertop or fastened to the wall.

Batterboard A slat fastened horizontally to stakes at a foundation corner. Strings are run between batterboards to mark the perimeter of slabs or foundations.

Beam A large horizontal support member, often made of doubled 2× or 4× stock and secured to posts.

Bluestone A dark, blue-gray granite.

Board Any piece of lumber that is less than 2 inches thick and more than 3 inches wide.

Boulder A large stone, usually round or egg-shaped, weathered and worn smooth.

Building codes Community ordinances governing the manner in which a home or other structure may be constructed or modified. Most codes deal primarily with fire and health concerns and have separate sections relating to electrical, plumbing, and structural work. See also zoning.

C-F

Capstone The top course of stone on a wall or the flat top stone on a pillar or post.

Carcass The boxlike outer body or framework of a cabinet.

Dimension lumber A piece of lumber that is at least 2 inches thick and at least 2 inches wide.

Dry-laid A stone patio or path laid without mortar, usually on a sand and gravel base.

Dry-stacked A wall constructed of stacked stones without mortar.

Fascia Horizontal trim attached to the outside ends of rafters or to the top of an exterior wall.

Fieldstone Smooth granite rocks, round or oblong. 6 to 24 inches in diameter, found on the ground or partially buried.

Flagstone Flat slabs of limestone, quartz, sandstone, or other kinds of stone. The slabs are often large but are easy to split. Flagstone is used for paths, patios, walls, and other projects.

Flashing Thin metal barriers or layers, often preformed into bent shapes, used to divert water away from window and door openings and often interruptions in an exterior wall.

Footing A thick concrete support for walls and other structures buried below the frost line to prevent heaving when the soil freezes.

Framing The skeletal or structural support of a building.

Frost heave The lifting of a concrete slab or other structure from soil expansion due to freezing.

Frost line The maximum depth frost penetrates the soil during winter. This varies by region and determines the necessary depth for deck piers, foundations, and post footings.

Furring Lightweight wood or metal strips that even up a wall or ceiling for paneling. On masonry furring provides surface on which to nail.

G-L

Gable The triangular area on the end of a building's external wall located beneath the sloping parts of a roof and above the line that runs between the roof's eaves.

Grade (noun) The level of the ground at a project site. (verb) To change, level, or smooth the surface of the ground.

Granite Hard, natural, igneous rock that contains quartz and forms of crystalline feldspar.

Gravel Small, loose rocks. Natural gravel often comes from rivers; rocks are smooth and rounded. The rocks in crushed gravel, made by mechanically crushing larger rocks, are irregular and jagged.

Grout A thin mortar used to fill the joints between ceramic tiles; often colored to match or complement the tile.

Joist A horizontal framing member, set on its edge and spanning an open space below, that supports a floor or ceiling.

Ledger A horizontal framing member fastened to a wall to support a floor frame or the joists in a deck structure.

Limestone A versatile stone formed from the calcium carbonate in shells and other organic remains.

Lintel A load-bearing beam spanning an opening, such as a doorway or a fireplace.

M-P

Mortar A mixture of one part sand, one part portland cement, and enough water to make a thick paste; used to set stone for patios, walls, and other projects and as grout between stones.

Nominal dimension The stated dimensions of lumber or masonry components. In lumber, the nominal size reflects a rough-sawn product, so the dimensioned piece is smaller. In masonry units, the nominal size includes the mortar joint, so the brick or block alone is slightly smaller than stated.

Nonvitreous tile. Porous ceramic tiles used indoors in dry locations.

Paver Stone cut to a uniform size for use in paths or patios.

Pergola An open overhead structure designed to provide shade.

Pier A concrete pedestal that supports deck posts and other structural components; usually set on top or cast as an integral part of a poured concrete footing.

Post-and-beam A basic building method that uses a few heavy posts and beams to support an entire structure. Contrasts with stud framing.

Pressure-treated wood Lumber (typically southern yellow pine) that has been saturated with preservative compounds to resist insects and fungal decay. It is used for deck structures, sill plates, and other outdoor applications.

Purlin A horizontal piece in a cabinet, wall, or roof.

Q-Z

Rafters Parallel framing members that support a roof.

Retaining wall A wall constructed to prevent soil behind it from sliding down a slope.

Sandstone A sedimentary rock that usually contains quartz sand. Flagstones are often large pieces of sandstone.

Screed A straightedge, often a 2×4 or 2×6, used to level concrete as it is poured into a form and to level the sand base in a form. Also, the process of leveling concrete or a sand base.

Setback The distance from the edge of a structure to an adjacent property line, usually stated as a minimum requirement.

Slate Dense stone formed in nature by compression of sedimentary rock; flagstones are often large pieces of slate.

Stone tile Marble, granite, slate, and flagstone. Dimensioned (or gauged) stone is cut to uniform size. Hand-split (or cleft stone) varies in size.

Stud framing A building method that distributes structural loads to each of a series of relatively lightweight studs. Contrasts with post-and-beam.

Substrate A foundation layer of material upon which another material is installed or fastened.

Thinset mortar A common setting adhesive for ceramic tiles used to create a bonding layer between the substrate and tile.

Veneer A thin layer of decorative material, such as brick or stone, attached to the surface of a base material to serve as a facing.

Zoning Ordinances regulating the ways in which a property may be used in a given neighborhood. Zoning laws may limit where a structure may be located.

Index

Index

METRIC CONVERSIONS

U.S. UNITS TO METRIC EQUIVALENTS			METRIC UNITS TO U.S. EQUIVALENTS		
To Convert From	Multiply By	To Get	To Convert From	Multiply By	To Get
Inches	25.4	Millimeters	Millimeters	0.0394	Inches
Inches	2.54	Centimeters	Centimeters	0.3937	Inches
Feet	30.48	Centimeters	Centimeters	0.0328	Feet
Feet	0.3048	Meters	Meters	3.2808	Feet
Yards	0.9144	Meters	Meters	1.0936	Yards
Square inches	6.4516	Square centimeters	Square centimeters	0.1550	Square inches
Square feet	0.0929	Square meters	Square meters	10.764	Square feet
Square yards	0.8361	Square meters	Square meters	1.1960	Square yards
Acres	0.4047	Hectares	Hectares	2.4711	Acres
Cubic inches	16.387	Cubic centimeters	Cubic centimeters	0.0610	Cubic inches
Cubic feet	0.0283	Cubic meters	Cubic meters	35.315	Cubic feet
Cubic feet	28.316	Liters	Liters	0.0353	Cubic feet
Cubic yards	0.7646	Cubic meters	Cubic meters	1.308	Cubic yards
Cubic yards	764.55	Liters	Liters	0.0013	Cubic yards

To convert from degrees Fahrenheit (F) to degrees Celsius (C), first subtract 32, then multiply by $\frac{5}{9}$.

To convert from degrees Celsius to degrees Fahrenheit, multiply by $\frac{9}{5}$, then add 32.

Welcome Home

DECK & PATIO
[Design Guide]

Better Homes and Gardens

IDEAS & HOW-TO
Stone Landscaping

Better Homes and Gardens

INCLUDED with your purchase is a **1-YEAR** subscription to Better Homes and Gardens magazine

Paths · Steps · Patios · Walls

IDEAS & HOW-TO
Garden Structures

Better Homes and Gardens

INCLUDED with your purchase is a **1-YEAR** subscription to Better Homes and Gardens magazine

Gazebos · Arbors · Trellises · Pergolas

Expert **advice** + **inspiration** + **ideas** + **how-to** for designing, building, maintaining your home's beautiful exterior

ADT0293_0907